JÜDISCHES MUSEUM MÜNCHEN
JEWISH MUSEUM MUNICH

Dieser Katalog erscheint zur gleichnamigen Ausstellung
des Jüdischen Museums München vom 28. November 2007 bis 16. März 2008.

This book has been published in conjunction with the exhibition of the same title
organized by the Jewish Museum Munich from November 28, 2007 to March 16, 2008.

ÜBERSETZUNGEN
\ TRANSLATIONS
Georgia Hanenberg
Christopher Wynne

LEKTORAT
\ COPYEDITING
Janice Meyerson (English)

GRAFIK
\ DESIGN AND LAYOUT
Haller & Haller, Wien

GESAMTHERSTELLUNG
\ PRODUCTION
Peschke Druck, München

Die Deutsche Bibliothek verzeichnet diese
Publikation in der Deutschen Nationalbibliographie.
Detaillierte Angaben sind im Internet über
http://dnb.ddb.de abrufbar.

© 2007 Jüdisches Museum München
© 2007 Edition Minerva Hermann Farnung GmbH, München

Alle Rechte, auch diejenigen der Übersetzung,
der photomechanischen Wiedergabe und
des auszugsweisen Abdrucks, vorbehalten.

All rights reserved.

ISBN 978-3-938832-26-4

SAMMELBILDER **05** COLLECTING IMAGES

Emily D. Bilski

Die Kunst- und Antiquitätenfirma Bernheimer
The Art and Antiques House of Bernheimer

EDITION MINERVA　　　　　　　　　　MÜNCHEN 2007

SAMMELBILDER
\ COLLECTING IMAGES
Eine Ausstellungsreihe des Jüdischen Museums München
An exhibition series organized by the Jewish Museum Munich

IDEE UND KONZEPT
\ IDEA AND CONCEPT
Bernhard Purin

SAMMELBILDER [05]
Die Kunst- und Antiquitätenfirma Bernheimer
28. November 2007 bis 16. März 2008

COLLECTING IMAGES [05]
The Art and Antiques House of Bernheimer
November 28, 2007 to March 16, 2008

KURATORIN
\ CURATOR
Emily D. Bilski

MITARBEIT
\ CURATORIAL ASSISTANCE
Juliette Israël

KOORDINATION
\ COORDINATION
Verena Immler

AUSSTELLUNGSGESTALTUNG
\ EXHIBITION DESIGN
Architekt Martin Kohlbauer, Wien

REALISIERUNG
\ REALIZATION
Architekt Christian Koch, Nürnberg

AUSSTELLUNGSGRAFIK
\ EXHIBITION GRAPHICS
Haller & Haller, Wien

AUSSTELLUNGSPRODUKTION
\ EXHIBITION PRODUCTION
Wolfgang Wastian

LEIHGEBER
\ LENDERS
Sammlung Familie Bernheimer, Burg Marquartstein

Bayerisches Nationalmuseum, München
Deutsches Museum, München
Landesmuseum Württemberg, Stuttgart
Schweizerisches Landesmuseum, Zürich
Städtische Galerie im Lenbachhaus, München
Stadtmuseum München

DANK
\ ACKNOWLEDGMENTS
Barbara und \ and Konrad Bernheimer, Blanca, Felicia, Isabel
und \ and Dr. Teresa Bernheimer

Elke Albrecht-Messer
Dr. Helmut Bauer
Johannes Baur
G. Max Bernheimer, New York
Iris Bernheimer-Goodwin
Martin Bernheimer, New York
Berthold Bilski, New York
Dr. Ing. Dirk Bühler
Martina Eberspächer
Dr. Barbara Eschenburg
Dr. Wilhelm Füßl
Dr. Jonna Gaertner
Andreas Geiger
Dr. Winfrid Glocker
Dr. Bettina Gundler
Dr. Walter Hauser
Dr. Sabine Hesse, Stuttgart
Prof. Dr. Wilhelm Hornbostel, Hamburg
Dr. des. Christine Kitzlinger, Hamburg
Katharina Kling
Karl-Heinz Meissner
Prof. Dr. Gabriel Motzkin, Jerusalem
Sigrid Pallmert, Zürich
Klaus Peitzmeier
Dr. Hartmut Petzold
Edith Plöthner
Karola Rattner
Dr. Sigrid Sangl
Dirk Spath
Dr. Wolfgang Till

Inhalt
Contents

8 **Vorwort**
Foreword

12 EMILY D. BILSKI
Die Kunst- und Antiquitätenfirma Bernheimer
The Art and Antiques House of Bernheimer

50 SAMMELBILDER 05 COLLECTING IMAGES
Verzeichnis der Ausstellungsexponate
Checklist of Works Exhibited

58 **Bibliographie**
Bibliography

SAMMELBILDER 05 COLLECTING IMAGES

Vorwort
Foreword

VORWORT \ FOREWORD

Im Jahr seiner Eröffnung stellt sich das Jüdische Museum München mit einer achtteiligen Ausstellungsreihe vor, die eine der wesentlichen Aufgaben der Institution thematisiert: *Sammelbilder [01]–[08]* beleuchtet aus unterschiedlichen Perspektiven die Geschichte des Sammelns von Jüdischem von der Renaissance bis in die Gegenwart und stellt jüdische Sammlerpersönlichkeiten aus München vor. Eine während des gesamten, bis Frühjahr 2008 andauernden Zyklus fest installierte Informationsebene ermöglicht die Einordnung des aktuellen Ausstellungsthemas in größere Zusammenhänge und erlaubt Rückblicke und Vorschauen auf die anderen Themen und Schwerpunkte der *Sammelbilder [01]–[08]*.

Die fünfte Etappe der Ausstellungsreihe *Sammelbilder* spürt der Geschichte der Familie Bernheimer nach, die seit der Mitte des 19. Jahrhunderts bis heute den Kunst- und Antiquitätenhandel in München maßgeblich mitgestaltet und mitprägt. Wie viele andere Münchner Juden zogen die Bernheimers im 19. Jahrhundert von einer süddeutschen Landgemeinde in die Metropole an der Isar und bauten aus bescheidenen Anfängen auf der „Dult" und in einem Gewölbe in der Kaufinger Straße eines der bedeutendsten Geschäfte des Kunst- und Antiquitätenhandels in Europa auf. Die Wittelsbacher, Königs- und Fürstenhäuser aus ganz Europa, aber auch amerikanische Magnaten wie William Randolph Hearst zählten zum Kundenkreis der Bernheimers und das 1889 am Lenbachplatz errichtet „Palais Bernheimer" wurde zur ersten Adresse für auserlesene Kunst und Antiquitäten.

During its first year, the Jewish Museum Munich is celebrating its inauguration with an eight-part exhibition series, *Collecting Images [01]–[08]*, which highlights one of the museum's core functions—that of collecting. Starting with the Renaissance and reaching to the present day, *Collecting Images [01]–[08]* explores the history of collecting Judaica from different perspectives, and introduces prominent Jewish collectors from Munich. A special information section—which accompanies the *Collecting Images* series lasting through 2008—places each of these eight temporary exhibitions in a wider context and draws out connections between the themes and key points introduced in *Collecting Images [01]–[08]*.

The fifth exhibition in the *Collecting Images* series traces the history of the Bernheimer family, which has played a decisive role and greatly influenced the art and antiques business in Munich since the middle of the nineteenth century, and continues to do so today. Like many other Jewish families in Munich, the Bernheimers moved to the Bavarian capital from a rural community in southern Germany in the nineteenth century. From their modest beginnings at the "Dult" fair and from a vaulted basement in the Kaufingerstrasse, they went on to establish one of the most important art and antiques businesses in Europe. The Wittelsbachs and other royal households throughout Europe, as well as American tycoons such as William Randolph Hearst, were among the Bernheimers' customers. The Palais Bernheimer, established in 1889 on the Lenbachplatz in Munich, became the best address for art and antiques of the highest quality.

Martin Kohlbauer
Entwurf für die Gestaltung der Ausstellung
Die Kunst- und Antiquitätenfirma Bernheimer
2007

Martin Kohlbauer
Sketch for the exhibition design
The Art and Antiques House of Bernheimer
2007

VORWORT \ FOREWORD

Mitglieder der Familie traten aber auch immer wieder als Sammler und als Stifter für Münchner Museen hervor. Die Ausstellung illustriert mit zahlreichen Leihgaben aus Familien- und Museumsbesitz die Geschichte dieser heute in München in vierter und fünfter Generation als Kunsthändler tätigen Familie, erinnert aber auch an Arisierung, Verfolgung und Emigration zwischen 1933 und 1945 und den Wiederaufbau nach 1945.

Dies verweist auf ein weiteres Anliegen der Ausstellungsreihe: *Sammelbilder* [01]-[08] erzählt auch die Geschichte des Raubes jüdischen Besitzes von der frühen Neuzeit bis ins 20. Jahrhundert und führt einmal mehr vor Augen, dass die Beschäftigung mit diesem Aspekt des Sammelns und die Suche nach Lösungen eine zentrale Aufgabe des Museums der Gegenwart ist.

München, im November 2007

Bernhard Purin
Direktor

Family members have always included collectors and donors to museums in Munich, and with numerous loans from family collections and museums, this exhibition illustrates the history of the Bernheimer family as art dealers in Munich, now in the fourth and fifth generation, while at the same time looking at the Aryanization, persecution, and emigration in the period between 1933 and 1945, and the rebuilding of their business after 1945.

This introduces a further focal point of the exhibition series: *Collecting Images [01]–[08]* also tells the story of the looting of Jewish property, from the early modern period into the twentieth century, and once again shows how dealing with this aspect of collecting and searching for solutions are among the central challenges facing museums today.

Munich, November 2007

Bernhard Purin
Director

Emily D. Bilski
Die Kunst- und Antiquitätenfirma Bernheimer
The Art and Antiques House of Bernheimer

Geschäftshaus der Firma L. Bernheimer, Lenbachplatz 3, nach seiner Vollendung 1890

Company building of the firm L. Bernheimer at Lenbachplatz 3, after its completion in 1890

DIE KUNST- UND ANTIQUITÄTENFIRMA BERNHEIMER \ THE ART AND ANTIQUES HOUSE OF BERNHEIMER

Ein englischer Tourist, der im Jahre 1914 mit der aktuellen Ausgabe des „Baedeker" in der Hand München besichtigt hätte, wäre sicher über kurz oder lang bei den imposanten Gebäuden am Lenbachplatz gelandet: „... an der Westseite das Bernheimer-Haus, im Barockstil von Fr. Thiersch (1889), zwischen der Deutschen Bank und der Darmstädter Bank."[1] Der Baedeker führte nicht weiter aus, worum es sich bei dem Bernheimer-Haus handelte; vermutlich war das Unternehmen Bernheimer inzwischen derart weltbekannt, dass sich eine Erklärung erübrigte.

In vielerlei Hinsicht ist die Geschichte der Firma Bernheimer, die mit Kunst, Antiquitäten und Innenausstattungen handelte, repräsentativ für das Schicksal anderer jüdischer Münchner Kunsthändler von der Mitte des 19. Jahrhunderts bis in das „Dritten Reichs". Juden aus Bayerisch-Schwaben, Franken und Württemberg zogen in der Hoffnung nach München, sich ein besseres Leben aufzubauen; und der eine oder andere wandte sich dem Kunsthandel zu. Viele gründeten Unternehmen, die dank der Kennerschaft, dem Weitblick und dem Pioniergeist ihrer Besitzer auf diesem Gebiet Weltgeltung erlangten. Aufgrund ihrer innovativen Geschäftsmodelle und internationalen Kontakte trugen sie viel zum Ruf Münchens als Kunststadt bei. Zu den Firmen, die das Familienunternehmen von Generation zu Generation weitergaben, gehörten auch die Bernheimers, und doch ist ihre Geschichte einzigartig – im Hinblick auf Art und Umfang ihrer Tätigkeit, ihre Beziehungen zu Mitgliedern des Königshofes, ihr intensives Engagement für Münchner Museen, und den Wiederaufbau des Unternehmens nach dem Zweiten Weltkrieg.

An English-speaking visitor to Munich guided by the 1914 edition of Baedeker's would have been directed to the grand buildings on the Lenbachplatz: "the Deutsche Bank and the Darmstädter Bank... and between them is the Bernheimer House built in the baroque style by F. von Thiersch."[1] Baedeker's offered no details on what was transpiring in the Bernheimer House; perhaps by then, the Bernheimer firm had become such a world-renowned institution that no explanation was needed.

In many respects the history of the Bernheimer firm, which dealt in art, antiques, and interior decoration, is representative of other Jewish art dealers in Munich from the mid-nineteenth century and through the period of the Third Reich. Jews migrated to Munich from towns and villages in Swabia, Franconia, and Württemberg looking to build a better life, and some gravitated to the art business. Many established firms that became international leaders in the field, distinguished by the connoisseurship, vision, and pioneering spirit of their owners, who developed new business concepts and fruitful international contacts, enhancing Munich's reputation as a city for art. Many firms were family-owned, passed down through several generations. Such was the case with the Bernheimers. Yet in the nature and scope of their business, their relationship with the Bavarian royal family, their intensive engagement with Munich's museums and their redevelopment of the firm in the years after World War II, the story of the Bernheimers is unique.

Ein Familienunternehmen

Zweimal im Jahr kam Meier Bernheimer (1801–1870) aus dem württembergischen Dorf Buttenhausen nach München, um in einem offenen Stand auf dem „Dult" genannten Jahrmarkt allerlei Tuch- und Modewaren feilzubieten. Aus diesen bescheidenen Anfängen sollte der wichtigste Kunst- und Antiquitätenhandel Deutschlands entstehen, gegründet von Meiers Sohn Lehmann (1841–1918). Dieser erwarb im Jahr 1864 von dem kurz vor dem Bankrott stehenden Robert Warschauer das Textilwarengeschäft an der Ecke Promenade-/Salvatorstraße. Hier verkaufte Bernheimer Kleiderstoffe sowie Damenkonfektion, wozu bald auch noch Möbelstoffe und Teppiche kamen. Über die folgenden Jahrzehnte expandierte die Firma Bernheimer stetig und erweiterte die angebotene Palette von Waren und Dienstleistungen immer mehr, so dass man sich gezwungen sah, in immer imposantere Räumlichkeiten umzuziehen.

Im Jahr 1870 zog Lehmann in ein Wohn- und Geschäftshaus in der Kaufingerstraße 17, wo er genügend Platz hatte, und das er später auch käuflich erwarb. Wohnung und Geschäft waren mit orientalischen Kunst- und Gebrauchsgegenständen sowie Teppichen ausgestattet, die Lehmann von seinen Einkaufsfahrten mitgebracht hatte, und es dauerte nicht lang, bis er diese Stücke auch seinen Kunden offerierte, wobei er in Anzeigen damit warb, auf „Orientteppiche" spezialisiert zu sein (Kat. Nr. 32). Im Familienkreis erzählte man sich, Lehmann habe Freunden, unter anderem dem Maler Franz von Lenbach (Kat. Nr. 29) und dem Baumeister und Bildhauer Lorenz Gedon,

A Family Business

Meier Bernheimer (1801–70), from the Württemberg village of Buttenhausen, came to Munich to sell fabrics from a stall at a fair known as the Dult. From these humble beginnings grew the most important art and antiques firm in Germany, founded by Meier's son Lehmann (1841–1918). In 1864, Lehmann Bernheimer acquired Robert Warschauer's textile business, which was facing bankruptcy, on the corner of Promenadestrasse and Salvatorstrasse. Here Bernheimer sold fabrics for clothing alongside ready-to-wear garments, and within a few years he added upholstery material and carpets to his offerings. Over the next decades, the Bernheimer firm expanded steadily, providing a wider selection of merchandise and services, which in turn required the firm to move to ever grander premises.

In 1870 Lehmann moved to a large space at Kaufingerstrasse 17, which he eventually purchased and used for both business and living quarters. Both were decorated with oriental objects and carpets that Lehmann had brought back from his buying trips; before long, he began to offer these artworks to his customers as well, advertising a specialty in "oriental carpets" (cat. no. 32). According to family lore, Lehmann brought ten carpets to Munich and showed them to friends, including the painter Franz von Lenbach (cat. no. 29) and the architect Lorenz Gedon. When Gedon purchased all of them on the spot, Lehmann realized that he had discovered a promising new market.[2] Whereas the Middle Eastern and Asian carpets and artifacts were initially purchased on European buying trips,

Franz von Lenbach (1836–1904)
Studie für das *Porträt Lehmann Bernheimers*, 1903
Öl auf Pappe
Städtische Galerie im Lenbachhaus, München
Kat. Nr. 29

Franz von Lenbach (1836–1904)
Study for the *Portrait of Lehmann Bernheimer*, 1903
Oil on board
Städtische Galerie im Lenbachhaus, Munich
Cat. no. 29

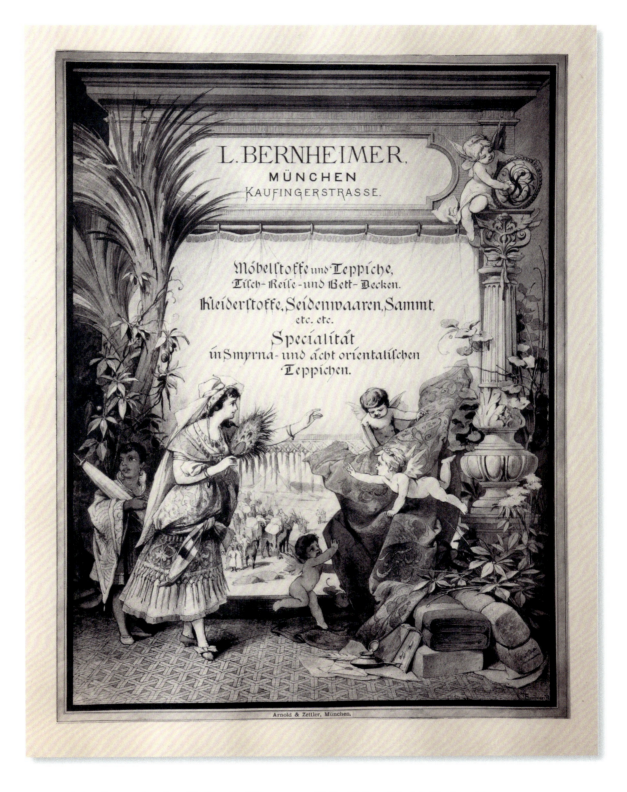

„L. Bernheimer, München, Kaufingerstraße. Möbelstoffe und Teppiche …"
Arnold & Zettler, München, 1879
Druck
Kat. Nr. 32

"L. Bernheimer, Munich, Kaufingerstrasse. Upholstery Fabrics and Carpets…"
Arnold & Zettler, Munich, 1879
Print
Cat. no. 32

Einweihung des italienischen Hofs des Palais Bernheimer durch Prinzregent Luitpold
München, 1910
Fotografie
Sammlung Familie Bernheimer, Burg Marquartstein
Kat. Nr. 33

Dedication of the Italian Court in the Bernheimer Palais by Prince Regent Luitpold
Munich, 1910
Photograph
Bernheimer Family Collection, Burg Marquartstein
Cat. no. 33

zehn dieser Teppiche gezeigt; doch erst, als Gedon kurzerhand alle zehn kaufte, sei Lehmann klargeworden, welch ein vielversprechender neuer Markt sich hier auftat.[2] Hatte Bernheimer die Teppiche und Gegenstände aus dem Mittleren Osten und Kleinasien ursprünglich auf Reisen innerhalb Europas erworben, importierte er diese Ware später direkt aus dem Fernen Osten und dem Osmanischen Reich. Hochwertige asiatische Kunst und Kunstgewerbe aus „direktem Einkauf im Orient" – Teppiche, Textilien, Keramik und Plastiken aus Japan, China, Indien und Siam – wurden zu einem der Markenzeichen, mit denen sich die Firma Bernheimer im Kunsthandel internationales Ansehen erwarb.

Mit der Erweiterung des Warenangebots kam auch die offizielle Anerkennung des bayerischen Herrscherhauses, das inzwischen zu seinen wichtigsten Kunden gehörte: 1882 ernannte König Ludwig II. Lehmann zum Kgl.-Bayerischen Hoflieferanten, und 1884 zum ersten Kgl.-Bayerischen Kommerzienrat. Ebenfalls 1884 tat Lehmann den entscheidenden Schritt und verkaufte seinem Bruder Leopold, der ein Geschäft in Ulm betrieb, seinen gesamten Lagerbestand an Damenkonfektion. Mit den neuen

Bernheimer eventually imported these items directly from the Far East and cities in the Ottoman Empire. High-quality Asian art—carpets, textiles, ceramics, and sculpture—from Japan, China, India, and Siam, "purchased directly in the Orient," became one way in which Bernheimer distinguished itself in the art market.

As Lehmann expanded the range of merchandise, he was officially recognized by the Bavarian Crown, which had become an important client: in 1882, he was appointed purveyor to the Royal Bavarian Court by King Ludwig II, and in 1884, he was named the first Royal Bavarian Councilor of Commerce. Also in 1884, Lehmann took the decisive step of selling off his entire stock of fabrics for women's fashion to his older brother Leopold, who had a business in Ulm. By concentrating on textiles for upholstery and wall coverings, and then on furniture and other elements for interior design, Lehmann defined the firm's identity and direction.

To provide adequate space and a fitting setting for clients, in 1887 Lehmann acquired a site on the Maximilianplatz—the

Gobelinsaal im Haus Bernheimer

Gobelin Hall in the Bernheimer House

Schwerpunkten Möbelstoffe und Tapeten, die später durch antike Möbel und andere Komponenten der Innenausstattung ergänzt wurden, legte Lehmann den Grundstein für das Selbstverständnis und die künftige Ausrichtung des Unternehmens.

Um mehr Platz zu haben und seinen Kunden ein angemessenes Ambiente bieten zu können, erwarb Lehmann 1887 ein Grundstück auf dem später zum Lenbachplatz umbenannten Teil des Maximiliansplatzes. Das prachtvolle, bei Friedrich von Thiersch und Martin Dülfer in Auftrag gegebene Palais wurde am 10. Dezember 1889 von Prinzregent Luitpold eingeweiht, ein Indiz der engen Verbundenheit zwischen den Bernheimers und dem Hause Wittelsbach.

Für den anhaltenden Erfolg des Traditionsgeschäfts nicht minder wichtig als die Erweiterung des Angebots und der Ausstellungsräume war 1893 die Aufnahme der drei Söhne Lehmanns in das Unternehmen: Max (1870–1933), Ernst (1875–1956) und Otto (1877–1960). Mit einundzwanzig Jahren erhielt jeder Sohn Prokura, war also bevollmächtigt, selbstständig Einkäufe zu tätigen; mit fünfundzwanzig wurden alle drei zu gleichberechtigten

future Lenbachplatz. The magnificent "Palais" that Lehmann commissioned from Friedrich von Thiersch and Martin Dülfer was dedicated by Prince Regent Luitpold on December 10, 1889, a reflection of the close ties between the Bernheimers and the Wittelsbach royal house.

As important to the ongoing success of the firm as the expansion of its wares and showrooms was the induction into the business in 1893 of Lehmann's three sons: Max (1870–1933), Ernst (1875–1956), and Otto (1877–1960). At the age of twenty-one, each son was named a procurer, with the independence to buy on his own for the firm; at the age of twenty-five, each became a full partner. Having apprenticed at firms outside of Germany, they entered the family business with specific areas of expertise, connections abroad, and knowledge of foreign languages. The brothers divided up the countries where they bought for the firm, and each took responsibility for different aspects of the business. Max was in charge of purchases in England and Constantinople and specialized in carpets. Ernst bought in France; he ran the fabric division and oversaw internal financial matters including bookkeeping and tax issues. Otto concentrated on purchases

Auswahl von Zierleisten
die in der Gestaltung von Inneneinrichtungen eingesetzt werden konnten.
Sammlung Familie Bernheimer, Burg Marquartstein
Kat. Nr. 26

Selection of Decorative Moldings
For use in interiors designed by the Bernheimer firm
Bernheimer Family Collection, Burg Marquartstein
Cat. no. 26

Teilhabern. Aus ihrer Lehrzeit im Ausland brachten sie Fremdsprachenkenntnisse, nützliche Kontakte und spezifische Fachkenntnisse mit. Also teilten die Brüder die Länder sowie die Verantwortung für die verschiedenen Sachgebiete und Geschäftsbereiche unter sich auf. Max war zuständig für Einkäufe in England und Konstantinopel und auf Teppiche spezialisiert. Ernst kaufte in Frankreich ein, leitete die Stoffabteilung und kümmerte sich außerdem um die Finanzen, einschließlich Buchhaltung und Steuerangelegenheiten. Otto hatte Italien und Spanien übernommen, und legte den Schwerpunkt auf antike Möbel, italienische Textilien, frühe spanische Teppiche, historische Architekturteile und Kunstwerke.[3] Um die Ausstellungsräume am Lenbachplatz zu bestücken und die immer zahlreicher strömende Kundschaft zu befriedigen, mussten Unmengen an Ware herangeschafft werden. In seinen Erinnerungen erzählt Otto, wie er in Verona einmal an einem einzigen Nachmittag 100 Renaissance-Truhen erstand (*Kat. Nr. 6*).[4]

in Italy and Spain, with emphasis on furniture, Italian textiles, and early Spanish carpets, architectural elements, and artworks.[3] Vast quantities of objects were required to fill the Lenbachplatz showrooms and satisfy a growing clientele. Otto recalled one afternoon in Verona during which he purchased 100 renaissance chests (*cat. no. 6*).[4]

Despite several setbacks—chief among them a fire in 1897, after which the prince regent offered Bernheimer the use of royal barracks as temporary storage during the rebuilding—the business continued to develop. Once again, more space was required. The houses at Ottostrasse 13 and 14 at the back of the edifice at Lenbachplatz 3 were acquired to provide more storage space; in 1908–09, a new building was erected on the Ottostrasse site.[5] Friedrich von Thiersch designed an Italian courtyard, inspired by the Bargello in Florence,[6] to showcase Renaissance stone sculpture, fountains, and architectural elements, which

Trotz einiger Rückschläge – vor allem ein Feuer im Jahr 1879, nach dem der Prinzregent den Bernheimers die königlichen Regimentskasernen als Zwischenlager zur Verfügung stellte – florierte das Geschäft weiterhin, so dass abermals mehr Platz geschaffen werden musste. Die hinter dem Gebäude am Lenbachplatz gelegenen Häuser in der Ottostraße 13 und 14 waren eigentlich als zusätzlicher Lagerraum hinzugekauft worden, doch entstand zwischen 1908 und 1909 auf diesem Grundstück ein Neubau:[5] ein von Friedrich von Thiersch entworfener Bau mit einem vom Bargello-Palast in Florenz[6] inspirierten „italienischen Hof" zur Präsentation von Steinskulpturen und -gefäßen, Brunnen, Bauteilen und Zierrat der Renaissance; im Jahr 1910 wurde der Hof in Anwesenheit des Prinzregenten Luitpold (*Kat. Nr. 33*) eingeweiht. Prunkstück des neuen Gebäudes war der Gobelinsaal, im Einklang mit der damals herrschenden Mode ganz mit Kunstgegenständen, Möbeln (*Kat. Nr. 5*) und Tapisserien aus der italienischen Renaissance ausgestattet. Diese historische Ausstattung war allerdings mit hochmodernem Errungenschaften kombiniert, darunter sechzehn elektrische Winden zum Hochziehen und Herunterlassen der Gobelins, eine aus alten italienischen Holzpaneelen gezimmerte Galerie sowie eine Kassettendecke, in deren einzelne Felder Glühlampen eingelassen waren.[7] Über den Türen nach Florentiner Vorbild prangte ein Relief mit dem Portrait des Prinzregenten in der mittelalterlichen Tracht eines Hubertusritters. Prinz Konstantin fasste den überwältigenden Gesamteindruck in die Worte: „Hier ist nicht mehr München. Hier ist Florenz in seiner Glanzzeit."[8]

Im Dienst einer internationalen Kundschaft

Bernheimer war international zu einem der führenden Kunst- und Antiquitätenhändler aufgestiegen. Zu seinen Kunden gehörten fast der gesamte europäische Hochadel, amerikanische

was dedicated in the presence of the prince regent in 1910 (*cat. no. 33*). The jewel in the new building was the "Gobelin Hall," inspired by the current fashion for art objects, furniture (*cat. no. 5*), and tapestries from the Italian Renaissance. Featuring Renaissance-style decor in the context of modern conveniences, the large room included sixteen built-in electric hoists to raise and lower the tapestries, a balcony of antique Italian wood panels, and a Renaissance coffered ceiling with electric lights embedded within the individual panels.[7] A relief portrait of Prince Regent Luitpold, in the medieval costume of a knight of Hubertus, crowned the large doors modeled on Florentine prototypes. The total effect was described by Prince Konstantin of Bavaria: "This place is not Munich any more. This is Florence at her time of splendor."[8]

Serving an International Clientele

Bernheimer had become a leading international purveyor of art and antiques. Clients included most of the royal families of Europe, aristocrats, American and European industrialists and plutocrats, diplomats, members of the haute bourgeoisie, and a host of successful scientists, university professors, artists, musicians, and writers. The carriages of the German railway system were outfitted in fabrics from Bernheimer. New York architect Stanford White bought at Bernheimer the objects and antiques that decorated the homes of the American Gilded Age,[9] and American newspaper magnate William Randolph Hearst purchased crates of art and antiques for his castle at San Simeon in California.

The Bernheimer firm understood the advantage of providing exceptional service, through designing and supplying complete interiors. Clients went to Bernheimer to outfit an entire room

und europäische Industrielle und Finanzaristokratie, Diplomaten, Angehörige des Großbürgertums, Dichter- und Malerfürsten sowie eine Vielzahl erfolgreicher Komponisten, Professoren und Wissenschaftler. Die deutsche Eisenbahngesellschaft ließ ihre Waggons natürlich mit Stoffen von Bernheimer ausstatten. Und auch die Kunstobjekte und Antiquitäten, mit denen der New Yorker Architekt Stanford White seine Häuser in der industriellen Blütezeit der USA ausstaffierte, stammten von Bernheimer;[9] sogar der amerikanische Zeitungsmagnat William Randolph Hearst bestellte kistenweise Kunst und Antiquitäten für sein Schloss in San Simeon in Kalifornien.

Die Firma Bernheimer hatte früh die Überlegenheit außerordentlicher Dienstleistungen erkannt und entwarf und lieferte daher Komplettausstattungen. Man ging zu Bernheimer, um sich ein Zimmer, manchmal auch eine ganze Wohnung oder ein Haus, komplett einrichten und dekorieren zu lassen: Es gab alle Arten von Stilmöbeln (*Kat. Nr. 24, 25, 28*), dazu Bezugstoffe für Sitzmöbel, Vorhänge und Tapeten (*Kat. Nr. 23*); Teppiche, Wandbehänge und Dekorationsstoffe, Gemälde, Plastiken und alle Arten von Raumdekor; Türen, Kamine, und sogar Zierleisten (*Kat. Nr. 26*) ebenso wie Tür- und Möbelgriffe (*Kat. Nr. 27*). Um nur zwei Beispiele zu nennen: Die Industriellenfamilie Krupp bestellte im September 1914 mehrere Interieurs für die Villa Hügel in Essen, darunter ein Arbeitszimmer mit einem karyatidenverzierten offenen Holzkamin und einem Louis XV-Tisch;[10] und im Dezember desselben Jahres ließ die Gräfin Zeppelin ihr Schloss von oben bis unten völlig neu einrichten und ausstaffieren.[11]

Hauseigene Zeichner und Architekten fertigten Aquarellentwürfe an, damit sich die Kunden eine Vorstellung von dem fertigen Raum machen konnten (*Kat. Nr. 19-22*). Im Hauptgeschäft gab es extra einen Raum mit beweglichen Zwischenwänden, mit denen das Personal jede gewünschte Raumgröße simulieren konnte. So

and sometimes a complete home: all types of furniture (*cat. nos. 24, 25, 28*), along with fabric for upholstery, curtains, and wall coverings (*cat. no. 23*); carpets, tapestries, paintings, sculpture, and decorative arts; doorways, fireplaces, and even interior moldings (*cat. no. 26*), door and furniture handles (*cat. no. 27*). To give two examples: the Krupp family of industrialists ordered several rooms for their Villa Hügel in Essen, including a study with wood fireplace decorated with caryatids and a Louis XV table in September 1914;[10] and in December of that year, Countess Zeppelin ordered a complete redecoration of her castle.[11]

Designers and architects employed by the firm produced watercolor renderings that conveyed to customers what a finished room might look like (*cat. nos. 19–22*). The firm's headquarters boasted a special room with movable screens, where the staff could simulate the dimensions of any given space: a newly decorated room and all its contents could be created on site for a prospective buyer. If the client was too busy to travel to Munich, Bernheimer would make house calls. Ernst Bernheimer assembled an entire salon—including carpets and furniture—and transported it to the Kassel home of the Hentschels, owners of Germany's leading locomotive factory, for their approval.[12]

Bernheimer's approach dovetailed with the prevailing taste of the time. With industrialization and mass production, the original, antique, handmade object with a historical provenance obtained a new aura; yet most collectors acquired objects in order to decorate their homes rather than to build a specialized collection for its own sake. The historicism of the period favored decors that imitated previous artistic styles or that integrated authentic elements from the past into contemporary interiors. Entire rooms were usually designed in one historical style; often the dining room and the study were outfitted in a Renaissance style, and the living room in French rococo.[13] Bernheimer could offer

DIE KUNST- UND ANTIQUITÄTENFIRMA BERNHEIMER \ THE ART AND ANTIQUES HOUSE OF BERNHEIMER

Entwurf der Einrichtungsabteilung des Hauses Bernheimer
München, vor 1938
Tempera
Sammlung Familie Bernheimer, Burg Marquartstein
Kat. Nr. 20

Design for an Interior by Bernheimer's Furnishings Department
Munich, before 1938
Tempera
Bernheimer Family Collection, Burg Marquartstein
Cat. no. 20

Entwurf für eine private Kappelle
durch die Einrichtungsabteilung des Hauses Bernheimer
München, vor 1938
Aquarell und Collage auf Pappe
Sammlung Familie Bernheimer, Burg Marquartstein
Kat. Nr. 21

Design for a Private Chapel
by Bernheimer's Furnishings Department
Munich, before 1938
Watercolor and collage on board
Bernheimer Family Collection, Burg Marquartstein
Cat. no. 21

war es möglich, für einen potentiellen Käufer ein Zimmer mit der neuen Austattung, einschließlich sämtlicher Einrichtungsgegenstände, an Ort und Stelle entstehen zu lassen. War der Kunde zu beschäftigt, um nach München zu kommen, kam die Firma zum Kunden nach Hause. Ernst Bernheimer stellte einmal einen kompletten Salon samt Teppichen und Mobiliar zusammen und transportierte ihn zur Ansicht nach Kassel zum Domizil der Familie Henschel – den führenden Lokomotivenherstellern in Deutschland.[12]

Bernheimers Herangehensweise traf genau den Zeitgeschmack. Mit zunehmender Industrialisierung und Massenproduktion hatte das alte, handwerklich gefertigte Original aus einer anderen Epoche einen neuen Nimbus erlangt; allerdings wurden die meisten Sammlerstücke als Zierde für das eigene Heim erworben, und nicht in erster Linie, um eine Sammlung aufzubauen. Wegen des herrschenden Historizismus fanden vor allem solche Einrichtungen Anklang, die den Stil früherer Epochen imitierten oder alte Originale in moderne Interieurs integrierten. Jedes Zimmer wurde gewöhnlich in jeweils einem bestimmten Stil gehalten. Das Ess- und das Arbeitszimmer waren oft im Renaissancestil eingerichtet, während man für den Salon französisches Rokkoko bevorzugte.[13] Bernheimer hatte zwar Originalexemplare im Angebot, konnte aber auch, wenn das Gewünschte nicht zur Verfügung stand, in den hauseigenen Werkstätten alles herstellen, um den Gesamteindruck des Echten zu schaffen. Die Einbeziehung von Originalen in ein neues Gesamtbild könnte man als eine Art Collage avant le lettre bezeichnen, was im Entwurf für die Privatkapelle eines Bernheimer-Kunden sehr schön zum Ausdruck kommt (*Kat. Nr. 21*): Die beabsichtigte Gestaltung von Decke und Säulen ist mit Bleistift und blauer Wasserfarbe skizziert, während Bänke und ein Altarbild als Fotografien auf das Blatt montiert sind.

original objects and architectural elements, and if they were not available, an appropriate mise-en-scène could be completed in the firm's workshops. The integration of authentic fragments into a new totality represented a form of collage, a process evident from the design for a private chapel created for a Bernheimer client (*cat. no. 21*): photographs of the pews and of an altarpiece are glued onto the page, while Bernheimer's architect has suggested a treatment for ceiling and columns in pencil and blue wash.

Museums in Germany, other parts of Europe, and the United States turned to Bernheimer for art and antiques and for the high-quality fabrics used for covering the walls and cases in exhibition galleries, as well as for special ceremonies. For example, Bernheimer provided the decorations for the festive cornerstone-laying ceremony of the Deutsches Museum (1907) in the presence of the Bavarian prince regent and the German emperor. Just before the outbreak of World War I, the Metropolitan Museum of Art in New York acquired an entire collection of important ecclesiastical textiles:[14] "a wide variety of church needlework, among which are a number of chasubles with embroidered orphreys. The most important of the group, however, are a superb sixteenth-century cope and a chasuble in cloth of gold."[15]

Belegschaft der Firma Bernheimer im italienischen Hof des Palais Bernheimer
München, 1914
Fotographie
Erste Reihe sitzend von Links:
Ernst, Lehmann, Max und Otto Bernheimer
Sammlung Familie Bernheimer, Burg Marquartstein
Kat. Nr. 34

Personnel of the Bernheimer Firm in the Italian Court of the Bernheimer Palais
Munich, 1914
Photograph
First row, seated from left to right:
Ernst, Lehmann, Max, and Otto Bernheimer
Bernheimer Family Collection, Burg Marquartstein
Cat. no. 34

Museen in Deutschland, im europäischen Ausland und in den USA bezogen von Bernheimer neben Kunst und Antiquitäten auch kostbare Stoffe, die nicht nur als Verkleidung für Wände und Schaukästen in Galerien, sondern auch für besondere Feierlichkeiten verwendet wurden. Zum Beispiel lieferte Bernheimer den Festschmuck für die Grundsteinlegung des Deutschen Museums (1907) in Anwesenheit des bayerischen Prinzregenten und des deutschen Kaisers. Kurz vor Ausbruch des Ersten Weltkriegs erwarb das Metropolitan Museum of Art in New York eine vollständige Sammlung bedeutender Kirchentextilien:[14] „… eine große Auswahl an handgefertigten liturgischen Textilien, darunter mehrere Messgewänder mit Goldstickerei. Am wertvollsten sind aber ein prächtiges Chorhemd aus dem sechzehnten Jahrhundert und eine golddurchwirkte Kasel."[15]

Krieg, Revolution und Inflation

Am Vorabend des Ersten Weltkrieges beschäftigte das Unternehmen 115 Mitarbeiter und Mitarbeiterinnen.[16] Mit einigem Einfallsreichtum gelang es, die Firma trotz mancher Schwierigkeiten heil über die Kriegsjahre zu retten. Da man keine Kunst mehr importieren konnte, suchte man eben innerhalb Deutschlands nach neuen Objekten. Im Jahr 1916 erwarben sie Bernheimers eine Seidenkunstweberei, damit sie mangels Nachschub aus dem Ausland ihre eigenen hochwertigen Seidenstoffe wie Damast, Brokat und Samt herstellen konnten.[17]

War, Revolution, and Inflation

On the eve of World War I, the firm employed 115 men and women.[16] Despite difficulties, the firm managed to weather the war years because of its innovativeness. Since artworks could not be imported, the Bernheimers sought new items in Germany. In 1916, they acquired a silk weaving mill in order to manufacture their own high-quality silk textiles—damask, brocade, velvet—during a period in which it was impossible to import fabrics from abroad.[17]

Lehmann Bernheimer died in May 1918 (*cat. no. 30*). Management of the business passed to his three sons. Despite Germany's defeat, the Bavarian revolution, and rampant inflation, the business prospered. Buyers were eager to invest their German marks, which kept losing value, in more permanent assets such as art and antiques. Clients from abroad were able to take advantage of the relatively low prices of goods priced in marks. With the stabilization of the mark, the attractiveness of art as a hedge against inflation diminished and foreigners no longer saw advantages to buying in Germany. In an attempt to find a solution to this problem, the Bernheimers opened a branch in Lucerne, Switzerland (as had other Munich art dealers, namely Heinemann and Thannhauser), which operated during the summer months only, to cater to wealthy American vacationers. The Swiss branch, managed by the next generation to enter the business—Paul (1910–2002), son of Ernst; and Ludwig

Im Mai 1918 starb Lehmann Bernheimer (*Kat. Nr. 30*) und die Geschäftsführung ging in die Hände seiner drei Söhne über. Obwohl der Krieg verloren war, in Bayern die Revolution und in ganz Deutschland Inflation herrschte, gedieh das Geschäft prächtig. Auf Grund der rasant steigenden Inflation versuchten viele, ihr Geld in wertbeständige Vermögen wie Kunst und Antiquitäten anzulegen, während ausländische Abnehmer davon profitierten, dass der Preis der Waren in Mark relativ niedrig lag. Als sich die Mark allmählich erholte, ließ auch der Reiz von Kunstkäufen als Absicherung gegen die Inflation nach, und im Ausland sah man keinen Vorteil mehr darin, in Deutschland einzukaufen. Um diese mißliche Lage in den Griff zu bekommen eröffneten die Bernheimers eine Filiale im schweizerischen Luzern (wie andere Münchner Kunsthändler, unter ihnen Heinemann und Thannhauser), die nur in den Sommermonaten in Betrieb genommen wurde, da sie vor allem für wohlhabende amerikanische Feriengäste gedacht war. Geleitet von Vertretern der nachrückenden Generation – Paul (1910–2002), ein Sohn von Ernst, und Ottos Sohn Ludwig (1906–1967) – hatte die Schweizer Niederlassung zudem den Vorteil, dass angesichts der zunehmenden Unberechenbarkeit der politischen Lage in Deutschland wertvolles Inventar außer Landes gebracht werden konnte. Die Kunden blieben jedoch unglücklicherweise aus, und das gesamte Unterfangen wurde nach nur zwei Sommern als „Fiasko" aufgegeben.[18] In diesen schwierigen Jahren musste Bernheimer viele seiner herausragendsten textilen Stücke bei Christie's in London versteigern lassen, um das nötige Betriebskapital aufbringen zu können.

Wie andere deutsche Geschäftsleute hatten auch die Bernheimers mit der wirtschaftlichen und politischen Instabilität zu kämpfen; als Juden hatten sie noch zusätzlich unter dem wachsenden Antisemitismus zu leiden. Obwohl die Bernheimers loyale Monarchisten mit engen persönlichen Beziehungen zu den Wittelsbachern waren, warf man ihnen vor, mit den Kommunisten

(1906–67), son of Otto—offered the possibility of transporting valuable inventory out of the country in order to shelter it from Germany's increasing political volatility. Unfortunately, the customers never materialized; the entire endeavor, deemed a "fiasco," was closed down after two seasons.[18] To help raise cash during those difficult years, Bernheimer sold many of its most important textiles at Christie's in London.

Like other German business owners, the Bernheimers had to contend with endemic economic and political instability; as Jews, they had the added burden of increasing anti-Semitism. Though the Bernheimers were loyal monarchists with close personal relations to the Wittelsbachs, they were accused of being Communist sympathizers and supporters of Munich's "Räterepublik" (Soviet Republic), compelling the three brothers to place notices in the local newspapers in 1923 denying the rumor and threatening legal action against anyone making this claim.[19] When the bank run by Ernst Bernheimer's son-in-law went bankrupt in 1929, the Bernheimer family assumed responsibility for its debts, with the knowledge that failure to do so would have resulted in anti-Semitic agitation, which the family could ill afford.[20]

Under National Socialist Dictatorship

Upon assuming power in 1933, the Nazis undertook the systematic exclusion of Jews from German professional and economic life and the spoliation of their property. This was accompanied by a gradual, yet relentless, attack on the dignity and personal freedom of Germany's Jewish citizens. Signs identifying the Bernheimer firm as a Jewish business were affixed to the façade of Lenbachplatz 3; many customers stayed away, either because of Nazi sympathies or out of fear. In 1935,

zu sympathisieren und die Münchner Räterepublik zu unterstützen, so dass den drei Brüdern nichts übrig blieb, als 1923 mit einer Anzeige in der örtlichen Presse diesen Verleumdungen entgegenzutreten und jedem mit Klage zu drohen, der dergleichen verbreitete.[19] Als 1929 die von Ernst Bernheimers Schwiegersohn geleitete Privatbank in Konkurs ging, übernahm die Familie Bernheimer sämtliche Schulden, um der ansonsten zu erwartenden antisemitischen Hetze vorzubeugen.[20]

Unter nationalsozialistischer Herrschaft

Nach der Machtübernahme 1933 begannen die Nationalsozialisten damit, die Juden systematisch aus dem Wirtschaftsleben hinauszudrängen und sich ihre Besitztümer anzueignen. Dazu kam die schleichende, aber immer erbarmungslosere Erniedrigung der jüdischen Bürger und die Einschränkung ihrer persönlichen Freiheit. An der Fassade des Geschäftsgebäudes am Lenbachplatz verkündeten Schilder, die Besitzer seien Juden, und viele Kunden kamen nicht mehr, sei es, weil sie die Nazigesinnung teilten oder weil sie Angst hatten. Im Jahr 1935 verbarrikadierten SS-Leute das Gebäude – jedenfalls bis sich herausstellte, dass Otto Bernheimer Jahre zuvor zum mexikanischen Konsul ernannt worden war und es daher auch als Konsulat diente. Ironischerweise waren die prunkliebenden Nazis mit ihren Paraden der Garant dafür, dass es der Firma Bernheimer nicht an Aufträgen mangelte. Da es nur wenige Bezugsquellen für die Materialien gab, die sie für ihre pompösen Veranstaltungen brauchten, ließ man alles über Dritte, zum Beispiel Architekten oder andere Händler, von Bernheimer besorgen. Auch andere Käufer griffen auf Mittelsmänner zurück; allerdings erwähnt Ernst Bernheimer in seinen Erinnerungen einen Kundenkreis, der ihm die Treue hielt, Kunden (zu denen auch die Krupps gehörten), die es sich nicht nehmen ließen, persönlich zu erscheinen und sie moralisch zu unterstützen.[21]

members of the SS closed the business and prohibited anyone from entering the premises until the SS was informed that the building was also serving as the Mexican consulate, as Otto Bernheimer had been appointed Mexican consul several years earlier. Ironically, the Nazi love of pomp and parades ensured that the Bernheimers did not lack for business. As there were few sources for the textiles that these spectacles required, these were purchased from Bernheimer via third parties such as architects or other dealers. Other customers also resorted to middlemen to make their purchases, though Ernst Bernheimer later recalled loyal clients who continued to buy from Bernheimer and insisted on coming personally to make their purchases and show their support, among them the Krupps.[21]

The most notorious client during those years was Hermann Göring, who subverted the Nazi-imposed ban on frequenting Jewish businesses with a four-hour-long visit to the Bernheimer firm, eventually purchasing two carpets.[22] Though a crowd had gathered outside the entrance on the Lenbachplatz as word spread of Göring's presence, the authorities kept all mention of his shopping expedition out of the newspapers.[23]

Max Bernheimer had died in March 1933; Ernst and Otto considered selling the business, but apart from the difficulty of finding a buyer possessing the necessary financial resources as well as the knowledge and experience to handle such a complicated enterprise, they were understandably reluctant to give in to Nazi pressure. As Ernst recalled: "One does not easily give up a firm that has so much tradition and that, already in the third generation, has been built up with such effort and work."[24] Several members of this third generation of Bernheimers had, unlike their fathers, pursued university studies. Max's son Richard finished a doctorate in art history and immigrated to the United States in 1934. Otto's younger son, Kurt, also studied art history

Der berüchtigtste Kunde jener Zeit war Hermann Göring, der den Boykott jüdischer Geschäftsleute unterlief und sich vier Stunden lang bei Bernheimer aufhielt, um schließlich zwei Teppiche zu erstehen.[22] Vor dem Haus versammelte sich eine Menschenmenge, als sich die Nachricht von Görings Besuch herumgesprochen hatte, aber die Machthaber sorgten dafür, dass seine Einkaufstour in den Zeitungen mit keinem Wort erwähnt wurde.[23]

Im März 1933 war Max Bernheimer gestorben; Ernst und Otto dachten zwar daran, das Geschäft zu verkaufen, aber zum einen hätte man nur mit Mühe Käufer mit dem erforderlichen Kapital sowie genügend Wissen und Erfahrung für die Leitung eines so komplexen Unternehmens finden können; zum anderen widerstrebte es ihnen verständlicherweise, dem Druck der Nazis nachzugeben. Ernst formulierte es so: „Eine Firma mit so viel Tradition, und mit so viel Mühe und Arbeit und nun in der dritten Generation aufgebaut, gibt man nicht leicht auf."[24] Im Gegensatz zu ihren Vätern hatten mehrere Vertreter dieser dritten Generation eine Universitätsausbildung genossen. Richard, der Sohn von Max, promovierte in Kunstgeschichte und emigrierte 1934 in die Vereinigten Staaten. Ottos jüngerer Sohn Kurt studierte ebenfalls Kunstgeschichte, wurde aber von den Nazis daran gehindert, sein Studium abzuschließen. Ludwig, der ältere Sohn, promovierte mit einer Arbeit über die juristischen Aspekte von Kunstversteigerungen[25] zum Doktor der Rechte, und wurde 1937 Teilhaber der Firma – gemeinsam mit Paul, dem Sohn von Ernst, der in der Schweiz Welthandel studiert hatte und in verschiedenen Unternehmen in Italien, England und Amerika ausgebildet worden war.

Die Krise kam im Jahr 1938, in dem die Bernheimers – mit den Worten Ottos – „restlos, seelisch und finanziell, durch die Nazis vernichtet wurden".[26] In der Pogromnacht vom 9. November 1938 gingen die Schaufensterscheiben am Lenbachplatz zu Bruch. Paul,

but was prevented from completing his degree by the Nazis. The older son, Ludwig, received a doctorate in law, writing a thesis on legal aspects of the auction business[25] and, together with Ernst's son Paul—who had studied commerce in Switzerland and trained with a variety of firms in Italy, England, and the United States—became a partner in the firm in 1937.

The year 1938 was a turning point, during which, according to Otto, the Bernheimers "were completely destroyed by the Nazis, both emotionally and financially."[26] On the night of November 9–10, 1938, during the anti-Jewish pogroms known as "Kristallnacht," the glass windows of the Lenbachplatz gallery were broken. Paul, Ludwig, and Kurt Bernheimer were threatened by armed members of the Hitler Youth who came to their homes and extorted money;[27] they were subsequently arrested and sent to the Dachau concentration camp. Otto, who had been out of town, was sent to Dachau the next day. Because of pressure from the Mexican government, which threatened to arrest twelve prominent Germans in Mexico in retaliation, he was released within a few days;[28] the others remained incarcerated for several weeks. All were forced to sign over power of attorney for their property to a representative of the Nazi Party.[29]

The Nazi regime now began to confiscate systematically the family's personal possessions. Members of the Gestapo, together with accompanying "experts," compiled inventory lists of the paintings, sculpture, decorative arts, furniture, and other valuables in the homes of Otto (November 15 and 17), Ludwig (November 15), and Ernst (November 17), to which activity they assigned the euphemism of "securing cultural property." Most of the items were seized and transferred to an annex of the Bavarian National Museum and later to the Munich City Museum; several volumes belonging to Ludwig were transferred to the Bavarian State Library.[30] A Renaissance chest and two fragments of

DIE KUNST- UND ANTIQUITÄTENFIRMA BERNHEIMER \ THE ART AND ANTIQUES HOUSE OF BERNHEIMER

Zerstörungen am Hause Bernheimer nach der Pogromnacht, November 1938
Damage to the Bernheimer House after the "Kristallnacht" pogrom, November 1938

Lenbachplatz 3 mit Kriegsschäden, 1945
Lenbachplatz 3 with war damage, 1945

Ludwig und Kurt Bernheimer wurden in ihren Wohnungen von Mitgliedern der Hitlerjugend bedroht und mit Waffengewalt zur Herausgabe von Geld gezwungen;[27] anschließend wurden sie verhaftet und ins Konzentrationslager Dachau gebracht. Otto, der sich an diesem Abend nicht in München aufgehalten hatte, brachte man am Tag darauf ebenfalls nach Dachau; auf Druck der mexikanischen Regierung, die damit drohte, im Gegenzug zwölf prominente Deutsche in Mexiko zu verhaften, setzte man ihn jedoch wenige Tage später wieder auf freien Fuß.[28] Die anderen blieben mehrere Wochen lang in Haft, und alle wurden gezwungen, einem Vertreter der NSDAP die Vollmacht über ihren Besitz zu übertragen.[29]

Nun begann das Nazi-Regime damit, das persönliche Eigentum der Familie systematisch zu konfiszieren. Mit Hilfe von „Sachverständigen" erstellte die Gestapo Inventarlisten der Gemälde, Skulpturen, sonstigen Kunstobjekte, Möbel und aller anderen Wertgegenstände in den Wohnungen von Otto (15. und 17. November), Ludwig (15. November) und Ernst (17. November); diese Aktivitäten bezeichneten sie beschönigend als „Sicherstellung von Kulturgütern". Die meisten Stücke wurden beschlagnahmt, erst in ein Nebengebäude des Bayerischen Nationalmuseums und später ins Münchner Stadtmuseum gebracht; der Bayerischen Staatsbibliothek wurden eine Anzahl von Ludwigs Büchern übergeben.[30] Eine Renaissance-Truhe und zwei Fragmente deutscher Stickereiarbeit aus dem 16. Jahrhundert nahm das Bayerische Nationalmuseum in seinen Bestand auf.[31]

Entsprechend einer behördlichen Verfügung vom 12. November 1938, „zur Ausschaltung der Juden aus dem deutschen Wirtschaftsleben", wurde die Firma Bernheimer zum Ende des Jahres geschlossen.[32] Dank neuerer Forschungen wissen wir heute mehr Details über das komplizierte Verfahren der „Arisierung", in dessen Verlauf den Bernheimers ihr Unternehmen gestohlen wurde.

sixteenth-century German embroidery were accessioned by the Bavarian National Museum.[31]

According to an ordinance of November 12, 1938, "to eliminate Jews from German economic life," the Bernheimer firm was ordered closed by the end of the year.[32] Recent scholarship has detailed the complex process of the firm's "Aryanization," by which the Bernheimers had their business stolen from them.[33] It is a measure of the importance of the Bernheimer firm and its international reputation that the question of what to do with it was in dispute between the Ministry of Finance in Berlin and the local Munich authorities, especially Adolf Wagner, who served as Gauleiter (Nazi district leader) of Munich. The Ministry of Finance wanted to dissolve the business and realize the assets. Wagner wanted to acquire the firm for the Nazi Party in Munich; with Hitler's support, he was ultimately successful.[34] The firm L. Bernheimer was purchased by the Kameradschaft der Künstler (Fellowship of Artists), an organization established at Wagner's instigation in July 1938.[35] The day-to-day operation was run by Josef Egger, who had been employed by the Bernheimers since the 1920s. The purchase tender made it clear who the beneficiary of the theft of the firm would be: "It concerns a trusteeship acquisition for the N[ational] S[ocialist] D[emocratic] P[arty], which has the greatest interest in placing the management of this business under its control."[36] The Bernheimers received no compensation from the sale of the business, since the proceeds were deducted from fictive tax debts and the various penalties and punitive taxes levied on emigrating Jews, such as the "escape tax."

The Bernheimers began a desperate search for a safe haven and sought permission to leave Germany. In an act of pure extortion, Otto was forced to buy at an exorbitant price a run-down coffee plantation in Rubio, Venezuela, that belonged to relatives of

„Auf der Suche nach der verlorenen Zeit"
Otto Bernheimer auf der Titelseite der Zeitschrift „Der Spiegel"
25. Dezember 1957
Kat. Nr. 31

"In Search of Lost Time"
Otto Bernheimer on the cover of the periodical *Der Spiegel*
December 25, 1957
Cat. no. 31

de.³³ Bedeutung und internationaler Ruf der Firma Bernheimer lassen sich aus der Tatsache ermessen, dass das Finanzministerium in Berlin und lokale Behörden in München – namentlich der Gauleiter Adolf Wagner – im Streit lagen, was damit geschehen sollte. Das Finanzministerium wollte den Betrieb liquidieren und die Vermögenswerte veräußern, während Wagner die Firma lieber in den Besitz der NSDAP München gebracht hätte. Mit der Unterstützung Hitlers gelang ihm dies schließlich auch,³⁴ und die Firma Bernheimer wurde von der Kameradschaft der Künstler aufgekauft, einem im Juli 1938 auf Betreiben Wagners gegründeten Verein. Mit dem Tagesgeschäft betraute man Josef Egger, seit den Zwanzigerjahren Angestellter bei der Firma Bernheimer. Wer die tatsächlichen Nutznießer sein würden, machte der Kaufantrag unmissverständlich klar: „Es handelt sich um einen treuhänderischen Erwerb für die NSDAP, die das größte Interesse daran hat, diesen Geschäftsbetrieb unter ihren Einfluß zu stellen."³⁶ Die Bernheimers erhielten keinerlei Vergütung, da erfundene Steuerschulden sowie verschiedene auferlegte Bußgelder und Strafsteuern – wie zum Beispiel die „Reichsfluchtsteuer" – mit dem Erlös verrechnet wurden.

Nun stellten die Bernheimers den Antrag, das Land verlassen zu dürfen, und es begann die verzweifelte Suche nach einem sicheren Zufluchtsort. Otto wurde genötigt, Verwandten Hermann Görings eine heruntergekommene Kaffee-Plantage in Venezuela zu einem völlig überhöhten Preis abzukaufen – eine glatte Erpressung: Göring drohte damit, andernfalls werde kein Bernheimer das Land lebend verlassen. Als Teil der Abmachung musste Otto auch noch Görings Tante und ihren jüdischen Ehemann nach Venezuela mitnehmen und dort für sie aufkommen.³⁷ Im April 1939 verließen Otto und seine Familie Deutschland. Kurt (1911–1954) heiratete in Venezuela und gründete eine Familie. Nachdem Kurt durch tragische Weise ums Leben gekommen war, holte Otto dessen Witwe und ihre drei Kinder zu sich nach München.

Hermann Göring; the Nazi leader threatened that otherwise, no member of the Bernheimer family would leave Germany alive. As part of the deal, Otto was obliged to take with him Göring's aunt and her Jewish husband and to support them in Venezuela. Otto's family departed Germany in April 1939. Kurt (1911–54) married and had three children in Venezuela.³⁷ After Kurt's tragic death, his widow and children settled in Munich at Otto's behest.

Most members of the family managed to emigrate. Ernst Bernheimer, his wife, and handicapped son obtained visas to Havana, Cuba, in 1941, where Ernst died in 1956. Ernst's other son, Paul, with wife Luise and family left Germany in April 1939 for England and eventually settled in the United States, with the help of distant American relatives. They established an antiques business in Massachusetts; their son Martin (b. 1936) became a prominent musicologist and a Pulitzer-prize-winning music critic.³⁸ The widow of Max Bernheimer, Karoline, and her two sons also reached safety in the United States. Richard Bernheimer (1907–58) became a professor of art history at Bryn Mawr College. Franz (1911–97), an artist whose work is represented in many museum collections, immigrated to Israel in 1961.

Otto Bernheimers Wohnzimmer in der Ottostrasse.
Die beiden Bildteppich-Fragmente (Kat. Nrn. 10 und 11)
sind im Hintergrund über die beiden Türe erkennbar.

Otto Bernheimer's living room at Ottostrasse.
The tapestry fragments (cat. nos. 10 and 11) can be seen
in the background, hanging above the two doorways.

Otto Bernheimers Zimmer im Geschäftshaus
mit den Bildern seiner Eltern, von Lenbach gemalt (vgl. Kat. Nr. 29)

Otto Bernheimer's room in the company building with the
portraits of his parents painted by Lenbach (compare cat. no. 29)

Den meisten Familienmitgliedern gelang die Emigration. Ernst Bernheimer gelang es 1941, für sich, seine Frau und einen behinderten Sohn Visa nach Havanna zu beschaffen, wo Ernst 1956 starb. Sein zweiter Sohn Paul ging im April 1939 mit seiner Frau Luise und Familie nach England und ließ sich später mit Hilfe entfernter Verwandter in den USA in Massachusetts nieder, wo sie einen Antiquitätenhandel aufbauten; aus ihrem Sohn Martin (geb. 1936) wurde ein namhafter Musikologe und mit dem Pulitzerpreis ausgezeichneter Musikkritiker.[38] Max Bernheimers Witwe Karoline konnte sich und ihre zwei Söhne ebenfalls in den Vereinigten Staaten in Sicherheit bringen. Richard Bernheimer (1907–1958) wurde Professor für Kunstgeschichte am Bryn Mawr College; Franz (1911–1997), ein Künstler, dessen Werk in vielen Museen vertreten ist, machte 1961 Israel zu seiner Heimat.

Restitution, Remigration und Wiederaufbau

Nach der Niederlage Nazi-Deutschlands begann man in den West-Besatzungszonen mit der Rückgabe der geraubten Besitztümer an die jüdischen Eigentümer, ein Prozess, der ab den Fünfzigerjahren von der jungen Bundesrepublik fortgeführt wurde. So konnten sich die Bernheimers im Lauf der Zeit den größten Teil dessen, was man ihnen gestohlen hatte, zurückholen und ihre Firma erneut übernehmen (*Kat. Nr. 35*). Zwar eröffneten damals einige der ins Exil gegangenen Händler ihre Kunstgalerien wieder neu, doch führten sie die Geschäfte meist aus der Ferne. Dass Otto Bernheimer sich wieder in München niederließ, darf als ungewöhnlicher Schritt gelten. Angefangen von der Wiederherstellung des im Krieg schwer beschädigten Gebäudes am Lenbachplatz, spielte die Firma Bernheimer eine entscheidende Rolle beim Wiederaufbau der Stadt. Als Präsident des Bundesverbandes des deutschen Kunsthandels und einer der Initiatoren der Deutschen Kunst- und Antiquitätenmesse 1956 trug Otto

Restitution, Remigration, and Rebuilding

With Nazi Germany's defeat, the process of restituting stolen Jewish property began in the Western occupied zones, and was subsequently continued by the young Federal Republic of Germany in the 1950s. Eventually, the Bernheimers were able to recover most of the property that had been stolen from them and to reclaim their firm (*cat. no. 35*). While a number of exiled dealers chose to reestablish their galleries after the war, most chose to manage their businesses from afar. Otto Bernheimer took the unusual step of resettling in Munich. The Bernheimer firm played a crucial role in the city's rebuilding, beginning with the reconstruction of the gallery at Lenbachplatz, which had been badly damaged during the war. Otto served as president of the Federal Association of German Art Dealers and helped restore Munich's role in the international art market as an initiator of the German Art and Antiques Fair in 1956 (*cat. no. 36*). The sale at auction in December 1960 of art from his estate was a

Kasel
Deutschland, 15. Jahrhundert
Samt mit Stickerei
H: 110 cm; B: 72 cm
Museum für Kunst und Gewerbe Hamburg, # 1961.22
Ehemals Sammlung Otto Bernheimer

Chasuble
Germany, 15th century
Velvet with embroidery
H: 110 cm; W: 72 cm
Museum für Kunst und Gewerbe Hamburg, # 1961.22
Formerly Otto Bernheimer Collection

dazu bei, dass München wieder eine Rolle auf dem internationalen Kunstmarkt spielte. Die Versteigerung von Kunstwerken aus seinem Nachlass im Dezember 1960 geriet unter reger Anteilnahme der Presse zu einem Großereignis. Internationale Händler, Sammler und Museumsdirektoren waren gekommen, und die erzielten Preise lagen weit über den Schätzungen, so dass die Stadt München „ihre einstige führende Stellung auf dem Kunstmarkt zurückgewonnen" hatte.[39]

Nach dem Tod seines Vaters kehrte Ludwig nach München zurück, um den Gesellschafterposten bei Bernheimer zu übernehmen; als er 1967 starb, wurde Paul Bernheimer Gesellschafter. Im Jahr 1977 trat die vierte Generation in die Firma ein: Nach einem Intermezzo bei Christie's in London kehrte Konrad O. Bernheimer, Kurts Sohn und Ottos Enkel, nach München zurück und machte es sich zur Aufgabe, das Unternehmen zu modernisieren.

true "celebrity sale," attracting a flurry of press attention. It was attended by international dealers, collectors, and museum directors, achieved prices well beyond presale estimates, and established that Munich had "won back its former leading position in the international art market."[39]

Ludwig Bernheimer returned to Munich to become chairman of the firm after his father's death. When Ludwig died in 1967, Paul Bernheimer became chairman. In 1977, a fourth generation entered the business: Konrad O. Bernheimer, Otto's grandson and Kurt's son, returned to Munich after a stint at Christie's in London, and set about modernizing the business. He shifted focus away from decorating, textiles, and furnishings and concentrated on art and antiques. Though the decision was reached to liquidate the firm L. Bernheimer and sell the Lenbachplatz property in 1987, the Bernheimer name remains

Chanukka-Leuchter aus dem ehemaligen Besitz der Firma Bernheimer, dokumentiert von Theodor Harburger

Hanukkah lamp formerly in the collection of the Bernheimer firm, as documented by Theodor Harburger

Er verlagerte den Schwerpunkt auf Kunst und Antiquitäten; Innenausstattung und Stoffe traten in den Hintergrund. Trotz der 1987 getroffenen Entscheidung, die Traditionsfirma aufzulösen und die Liegenschaft am Lenbachplatz zu verkaufen, bleibt der Name Bernheimer fester Bestandteil des Kunstmarkts, dank Konrad O. Bernheimers Fine-Old-Masters-Galerie in München, seiner Übernahme von Colnaghi in London 2002, und seiner führenden Rolle im TEFAF (The European Fine Arts Fair) in Maastricht. Inzwischen ist die fünfte Generation im Kunstgeschäft angekommen: Blanca Bernheimer hat in der Galerie ihres Vaters eine neue Abteilung für moderne und zeitgenössische Fotografie aufgebaut.

Sammeln, Identität und Säkularisierung

Die meisten Händler sind zugleich Sammler. Sie haben umfassende Kenntnisse, einen geschulten Blick für Qualität und Zugangsmöglichkeit zu den schönsten Stücken, verfügen also über genügend Mittel und Kunstverstand, um bedeutende Sammlungen zu schaffen. Wie bei allen Sammlern läßt die Wahl der Objekte auf Charakterzüge, Sehnsüchte und Selbsteinschätzung schließen. Die von der Familie Bernheimer aufgebaute, bemerkenswerte Sammlung wertvoller Textilkunst (*Kat. Nr. 8–11*) zeugt von einer Begeisterung, die ihren Ursprung im Tuchhandel von Meier Bernheimer hat. Zu den Stücken, die aus emotionalen

a fixture on the international art market, on account of Konrad O. Bernheimer's Fine Old Masters gallery in Munich, his acquisition in 2002 of Colnaghi in London, and his leadership role in TEFAF (The European Fine Art Fair) in Maastricht. The fifth generation has joined the business: Blanca Bernheimer, a daughter of Konrad and Barbara, has built a new department of modern and contemporary photography.

Collecting, Identity, and Secularization

Most dealers are also collectors. With their vast knowledge, acute sense for quality, and access to the best objects, they have the means and talent to form great collections. As with other collectors, their personal choices reveal aspects of their personalities, aspirations, and sense of self. The Bernheimer family built one of the notable collections of textiles (*cat. nos. 8–11*), a passion that harkens back to the beginnings of the family firm in the textile trading of Meier Bernheimer. Among the items that were never sold for sentimental reasons was a Japanese Buddha (*cat. no. 3*), one of the first purchases made by Lehmann of Asian art in the 1880s.[40] That the family never lost sight of its Jewish roots is evident from its philanthropic activity in the Jewish communities of Buttenhausen and Munich, as well as in the works of Jewish ceremonial art that they owned. Among these objects, which were documented by Theodor

Werbeanzeige „L. Bernheimer München Lenbachplatz 3
(...) Direkter Einkauf im Orient"
Aus dem Katalog „Die Ausstellung von Meisterwerken muhammedanischer Kunst in München 1910"

Advertisement "L. Bernheimer Munich Lenbachplatz 3
(...) Direct Purchasing in the Orient"
In the catalogue *The Exhibition of Masterpieces of Islamic Art in Munich 1910*

Gründen nie verkauft wurden, gehörte ein in den 1880ern von Lehmann gekaufter japanischer Buddha (*Kat. Nr. 3*), eine seiner ersten Erwerbungen asiatischer Kunst.[40] Dass die Familie ihre jüdischen Wurzeln nie aus den Augen verlor, zeigt sich sowohl an ihren philantropischen Aktivitäten in München und Buttenhausen, als auch an den jüdischen rituellen Kunstobjekten in ihrem Besitz. Unter diesen, in den Zwanzigerjahren von Theodor Harburger[41] dokumentierten, Ritualobjekten befand sich auch ein großer Chanukka-Leuchter aus Messing, der der Jüdischen Gemeinde in München gestiftet wurde.

Ein Großteil der Textilkunstsammlung in Familienbesitz bestand aus zum liturgischen Gebrauch im christlichen Gottesdienst gefertigten Gewändern und Tüchern.[42] Die Vielzahl von Kirchentextilien, Kruzifixen und anderen Stücken christlichen Ursprungs in Otto Bernheimers Sammlung lässt auch die Behauptung, er habe „mit dem Christentum kokettiert"[43] ziemlich glaubwürdig erscheinen. Vielleicht waren Katholizität und sein geliebtes Bayerntum für ihn ja untrennbar verbunden: Gegen Ende seines Lebens hatte er auf dem Kaminsims eine Art Altar errichtet, auf dem Kruzifix, Madonnenstatue und Heiligenfiguren, gerahmte Fotos von Kardinal Faulhaber (Erzbischof von München), Prinzregent Luitpold, Oskar von Miller (Gründer des Deutschen Museums) und dem bayerischen Kronprinzen Rupprecht einträchtig nebeneinander standen.[44] Im Kontext seiner Sammlung beschwören die liturgischen Objekte die Sehnsucht nach einer

Harburger in the 1920s,[41] is a large brass Hanukkah lamp that was donated to the Munich Jewish community.

A large part of the family's textile collection consisted of items originally made for use in church ceremonies.[42] Otto Bernheimer's collection contained many ecclesiastical textiles, crucifixes, and other works with Christian content, lending credence to the suggestion that he "flirted with Catholicism."[43] Perhaps he saw Catholic culture as inherent to the Bavarian identity that was so dear to him: in his bedroom toward the end of his life, he created a kind of altar, with a crucifix, sculptures of a madonna and of saints, and photographs of Kardinal Faulhaber (archbishop of Munich), Bavarian Crown Prince Rupprecht, Prince Regent Luitpold, and Oskar von Miller, the founder of the Deutsches Museum.[44] Within the context of his collection, the Christian liturgical objects evoke nostalgia for a world of religious practice, but it is a world that would have been inaccessible to the collector. Susan Stewart writes about the ways in which a collection "destroys the context of origin" of the individual objects.[45] This is equally true of the way in which the Bernheimer firm and its clients took objects that had been bearers of religious meaning and integrated them into new, secular contexts. An example is the library that Bernheimer created for the Grand Duke Vladimir of Russia using paneling and the confessionals taken from a royal church at Chimay.[46] Indeed, reports on the auction of Otto Bernheimer's collection

versunkenen Welt gelebter Religion, aber dem Sammler selbst wäre diese Welt wohl verschlossen geblieben. Susan Stewart schreibt darüber, wie eine Sammlung die einzelnen Stücke „ihres ursprünglichen Zusammenhangs beraubt".[45] Gleiches gilt für die Art und Weise, wie die Firma Bernheimer und ihre Kunden die einst mit religiöser Bedeutung behafteten Gegenstände in eine neue, säkulare Umgebung einpassten; zum Beispiel schuf Bernheimer für den Großfürsten Vladimir von Russland eine Bibliothek unter Verwendung von Vertäfelungen und Beichtstühlen aus der Schlosskirche in Chimay.[46] Und tatsächlich fiel Berichterstattern bei der Versteigerung der Sammlung Otto Bernheimer auf, welch großes Interesse Vertreter des Klerus daran zeigten, Sakralgegenstände zu erwerben, um sie der Kirche zurückzugeben,[47] das heißt, sie in einen religiösen Kontext zurückzuführen.

Die Bernheimers und München

Die Bernheimers spielten und spielen im kulturellen Leben Münchens eine tragende Rolle. In ihrer Kunstgalerie fanden wichtige Ausstellungen statt, 1931 zum Beispiel eine Ausstellung von Khmer- und Siamplastiken[48], die im Burlington Magazine als „ein sowohl archäologisch wie künstlerisch bedeutendes Ereignis" gepriesen wurde.[49] Auch Ausstellungen der Münchner Museen profitierten von den Fachkenntnissen und Kunstschätzen der Firma – vor allem aus dem asiatischen und islamischen Bereich –, ganz besonders bei der Maßstäbe setzenden *Ausstellung von Meisterwerken muhammedanischer Kunst*, die 1910 in München gezeigt wurde. Sowohl Lehmann als auch Max Bernheimer gehörten dem Arbeitsausschuss für die Ausstellung an und steuerten eine große Anzahl Leihgaben bei: einen mittelalterlichen Bronzekessel aus West-Turkmenistan, eine Öllampe aus dem 12. Jahrhundert, drei weitere Gegenstände aus Metall, acht Teppiche und ein Stück türkischen Goldbrokatstoff

noted the interest on the part of the clergy in acquiring sacred objects in order to return them to the Church;[47] that is, to re-sacralize these objects by re-embedding them in a religious context.

The Bernheimers and Munich

To this day, the Bernheimers have occupied a leading position in Munich's cultural life. They organized significant exhibitions in their gallery, such as a 1931 show on Siamese and Khmer sculpture[48] that was lauded in *The Burlington Magazine* as "an important event from the archaeological as well as the artistic point of view."[49] Exhibitions mounted by Munich's museums benefited from the firm's expertise and holdings, particularly in Asian and Islamic art, most notably in the groundbreaking *Exhibition of Masterpieces of Islamic Art* held in Munich in 1910. Lehmann and Max Bernheimer both served on the exhibition's organizing committee and lent significantly to the show: a medieval bronze cauldron from west Turkestan, a twelfth-century oil lamp, three additional metal objects, eight carpets, and a seventeenth-century Turkish textile of gold brocade.[50] The exhibition was held in the Bavaria Park and included commercial pavilions and ancillary displays, in which the Bernheimers had a prominent presence: they contributed many objects to the exhibition of historical musical instruments, including items that were for sale, and they occupied seven rooms in the exhibition hall for art dealers; Max arranged for artisans from Smyrna and Istanbul to demonstrate carpet making on the exhibition grounds.[51]

Many objects in the permanent collections of Munich's museums passed through the hands of the Bernheimers. The relationship between the Bernheimers and the Deutsches Museum dates back to the family's friendship with the family of Oskar von Miller,

Wilhelm Gail
Fronleichnamsfest in der Frauenkirche, 1863
Öl auf Leinwand
Diözesan-Museum, Freising
Das Bild zeigt die Ausstattung der Münchener Frauenkirche mit dem Chor-gestühl nach der romantischen Restaurierung, um 1859/61 (vgl. Kat. Nr. 15)

Wilhelm Gail
Feast of Corpus Christi in the Frauenkirche, 1863
Oil on canvas
Diözesan-Museum, Freising
The painting shows the interior of Munich's Frauenkirche with the choir stalls, after the romantic restoration, c. 1859/61 (compare cat. no. 15)

aus dem 17. Jahrhundert.[50] Zu der Ausstellung im Bavariapark auf der Schwanthalerhöhe gehörten auch Verkaufspavillons und Sonderschauen, in denen die Bernheimers maßgeblich vertreten waren: Viele Stücke in der Ausstellung alter Musikinstrumente, darunter auch verkäufliche Exemplare, stammten aus deren Sammlung; und allein in der Halle für Kunsthändler belegten sie sieben der markierten Areale. Max hatte außerdem dafür gesorgt, dass Kunsthandwerker aus Smyrna und Istanbul auf dem Ausstellungsgelände die verschiedenen Techniken der Teppichherstellung demonstrieren konnten.[51]

Viele Exponate in den Sammlungen der Münchner Museen waren durch die Hände der Bernheimers gegangen. Ihre Beziehung zum Deutschen Museum entstand aus der Freundschaft zwischen ihrer Familie und der Oskar von Millers;[52] Lehmann war von Anfang an ein Förderer sowie Mitglied des ersten Museumsausschusses gewesen.[53] Zwischen 1905 und 1969 stiftete die Familie Bernheimer dem Museum über dreißig Kunstobjekte, unter anderem eine große antike Amphore, einen japanischen Steinbrunnen, das Mobiliar für die Galileo-Präsentation, eine marokkanische Öllampe (*Kat. Nr. 16*), einen zerlegbaren Ofen (*Kat. Nr. 17*) und eine skelettierte Standuhr (*Kat. Nr. 18*).

In den Sammlungen des Bayerischen Nationalmuseums finden sich viele – gekaufte, getauschte oder geschenkte – Kunstwerke Bernheimerscher Provenienz: Textilien, Teppiche, Holzschnitzereien sowie eine Anzahl historischer Interieurs, das Bernheimersche Aushängeschild. Am spektakulärsten ist wohl ein Kabinett aus dem 1910 abgerissenen Tattenbach-Palais in der Theatinerstraße mit seiner von Joseph Zächenberger auf Seide gemalten Wand- und Deckenverkleidung, die täuschend echt eine Gartenlaube nachbildet. Bernheimer hatte das als Meisterwerk gerühmte Kabinett vor 1932 erworben;[54] es fand Eingang in ein Verzeichnis von nationalen Schätzen im Besitz von jüdischen Kunsthändlern,

the museum's founder;[52] Lehmann was an early supporter and member of its first museum committee.[53] From 1905 to 1969, members of the Bernheimer family donated more than thirty objects, including a large ancient amphora, a Japanese stone fountain on the museum's grounds, the furniture in the display on Galileo, a Moroccan oil lamp (*cat. no. 16*), a portable oven (*cat. no. 17*), and a skeleton clock (*cat. no. 18*).

The Bavarian National Museum has in its collection many works with a Bernheimer provenance, acquired by purchase, exchange, or donation: textiles, carpets, woodwork, and a number of historical interiors, a Bernheimer hallmark. Perhaps most spectacular is the room from the Tattenbach Palais that stood in Munich's Theatinerstrasse until it was demolished in 1910. Joseph Zächenberger painted the decorative silk panels covering the walls and ceilings that simulate a garden bower. Bernheimer had acquired the room by 1932, when it was hailed as a masterpiece;[54] the room was included on a list of national treasures in the possession of Jewish Munich art dealers that was drawn up in 1935 for the Reich Chamber of Fine Arts by Hans Buchheit, then-director of the Bavarian National Museum.[55]

Joseph Zächenberger
Tattenbach-Kabinett
München, 1772–1779
Bayerisches Nationalmuseum, München

Joseph Zächenberger
Tattenbach Room
Munich, 1772–1779
Bayerisches Nationalmuseum, Munich

das Hans Buchheit, damaliger Direktor des Bayerischen Nationalmuseums, 1935 für die Reichskammer der Bildenden Künste erstellte.[55] Theodor Müller, nach dem Krieg neuer Direktor, legte besonderen Wert auf „echte Interieurs" und da er mit seinen knappen Mitteln das Tattenbach-Kabinett nicht erwerben konnte, holte er von den amerikanischen Dienststellen die Genehmigung zu einem Tausch mit Bernheimer ein.[56] Für das Kabinett und ein Figurenensemble aus Augsburg[57] erhielt Otto Bernheimer mittelalterliche Skulpturen sowie das Acquamanile (Kat. Nr. 7), das später ein Höhepunkt der Nachlassversteigerung werden sollte. Die Transaktion wurde weltweit als wichtiger Beitrag zum Wiederaufbau der Münchner Museumskultur nach dem Krieg gewertet.[58]

Noch ein anderes bedeutendes Stück aus der Baugeschichte Münchens fand dank Bernheimer Eingang in ein Museum, nämlich Teile eines Chorgestühls der Frauenkirche (Kat. Nr. 15), die 1958 als Schenkung an das Münchner Stadtmuseum gingen. Das zwischen 1858 und 1860 im Zuge einer Regotisierung entfernte Chorgestühl ging aus der Sammlung von Karl Theodor von Piloty, dem bedeutendsten Münchner Historienmaler, in den Besitz seines Schülers Eduard von Grützner über, der als Maler klerikaler Genre-Bilder bekannt war. Nach Grützners Tod erwarben die Bernheimers bei der Versteigerung seines Nachlasses zahlreiche Kunstwerke, eben auch dieses mit der Münchner Stadtgeschichte so eng verknüpfte Stück.[59] Es hatte fast drei Jahrzehnte im Keller des Palais' am Lenbachplatz geschlummert – weil der Geschmack sich geändert hatte und der Einbau von historischen Fragmenten in die Einrichtung nicht mehr gefragt war –, bis Otto Bernheimer erkannte, dass das Münchner Stadtmuseum der angemessene Platz für dieses Relikt wäre. Bei der Eröffnung einer Ausstellung zur 800-Jahrfeier der Stadt gab Museumsdirektor Max Heiß die Schenkung bekannt, derselbe Max Heiß, der als regionaler Leiter der Reichskammer der bildenden Künste eine unrühmliche Rolle bei der „Arisierung" des Kunsthandels gespielt hatte.

After the war, the new director, Theodor Müller, placed special emphasis on acquiring "authentic interiors," and as funds were too scarce to purchase the Tattenbach room, he secured the approval of American authorities to enter into a trade with Bernheimer.[56] In exchange for the Tattenbach room and a group of Augsburg sculptures representing the four seasons,[57] Otto Bernheimer received a group of medieval sculptures and the aquamanile (cat. no.7) that was later a highlight of the auction of his estate. The Tattenbach acquisition was recognized internationally as a significant step in the rebuilding of Munich's museum culture after the war.[58]

Another major piece of Munich's architectural history to enter a public collection courtesy of Bernheimer is a section of choir stalls from the Frauenkirche (Cathedral of Our Blessed Lady; cat. no. 15), donated by Otto Bernheimer to the Munich City Museum in 1958. The choir stalls had been removed from the cathedral as part of the re-Gothicizing renovation of 1858–60. One section passed from the collection of Munich's leading history painter, Karl Theodor von Piloty, to that of his student Eduard von Grützner, a Bernheimer client known for his genre scenes populated by clerics. After Grützner's death, the Bernheimers acquired many items at the auction of his estate, including this evocative piece of Munich history.[59] It seems to have languished in the basement at Lenbachplatz 3 for nearly three decades, as the taste for the integration of such fragments of medieval interior architecture had passed, until Otto Bernheimer discerned that the proper home for this magnificent, if much compromised, relic would be in the Munich City Museum. The gift was announced at the opening of an exhibition celebrating the city's 800th birthday by the museum's director, Max Heiß, who, as regional director of the Chamber of Fine Arts, had played a nefarious role in the process of "Aryanization" of Jewish art dealers in the Nazi period.

DIE KUNST- UND ANTIQUITÄTENFIRMA BERNHEIMER \ THE ART AND ANTIQUES HOUSE OF BERNHEIMER

Wenngleich die Geschichte der Familie Bernheimer in vieler Hinsicht als beispielhaft für die jüdischen Kunsthändler in München gelten kann, ist sie doch in einer Hinsicht einzigartig. Während die Kunstgalerien von Heinemann, Nathan, Thannhauser, Drey, Caspari, Helbing und anderer während der Nazi-Diktatur allesamt verschwanden, steht das Bernheimer-Palais am Lenbachplatz noch immer – und heute gibt es in der Brienner Straße, mitten in Münchens Galerienviertel, wieder ein Geschäft, das den Namen Bernheimer trägt.

If the Bernheimer story is in many ways emblematic of the place of Jewish art dealers in Munich's history, it is exceptional in one respect. Whereas the galleries of Heinemann, Nathan, Thannhauser, Drey, Caspari, Helbing, and others all disappeared during the Nazi tyranny, the Bernheimer House on the Lenbachplatz still stands and today there is a Bernheimer firm on the Brienner Strasse, in the heart of Munich's art gallery district.

1 Baedeker 1914, 249; Baedeker 1925, 24.
2 Bernheimer 1956, 16.
3 Ibid., 66.
4 Ibid., 36.
5 Ernst Bernheimer in: Familien- und Geschäftschronik 1950, 81, 83f., 88.
6 Ibid., 84.
7 Ibid., 86; Bernheimer 1956, 63.
8 Konstantin Prinz von Bayern 1956, 27.
9 Ernst Bernheimer in: Familien- und Geschäftschronik 1950, 98.
10 Privatarchiv Bernheimer, Geschäftsbuch K-M 88, fol. 29, 101.
11 Ibid., Geschäftsbuch T-Z 88, fol. 138ff.
12 Ernst Bernheimer in: Familien- und Geschäftschronik 1950, 99.
13 Gaehtgens 1993, 158, 160f.
14 Privatarchiv Bernheimer, Geschäftsbuch K-M 88, fol. 83. Ernst Bernheimer in: Familien- und Geschäftschronik, 92.
15 Morris 1915, 47.
16 Ernst Bernheimer in: Familien- und Geschäftschronik 1950, 111.
17 Ibid., 114.
18 Ibid., 136.
19 „Warnung", Stadtarchive München, ZA Pers. Bernheimer, Otto.
20 Ernst Bernheimer in: Familien- und Geschäftschronik 1950, 139, 167–71.
21 Ibid., 152–53.
22 Bernheimer 1956, 72–73; Otto Bernheimer in: Familien- und Geschäftschronik 1950, 178–79; Ernst Bernheimer in: Familien- und Geschäftschronik 1950, 152; Heuwagen 1987.
23 Friedländer 1997, 232–33.
24 Ernst Bernheimer in: Familien- und Geschäftschronik 1950, 153.
25 Bernheimer 1929.
26 Otto Bernheimer in: Familien- und Geschäftschronik 1950, 178.
27 Heusler, Weger 1998, 96–103, 107.
28 Otto Bernheimer in: Familien- und Geschäftschronik 1950, 180.
29 Ernst Bernheimer in: Familien- und Geschäftschronik 1950, 155.
30 Münchner Stadtmuseum – Registratur, Aktenvolut „Ehemaliger Judenbesitz".

31 Bayerisches Nationalmuseum, Inventarblätter 41/279, 41.299.a, b.
32 StadtA Mü, Gewerbeamt (GA), Abg. 7/12a Bernheimer; 13. Dez. 1938, Nr. 25414.
33 Schleusener 2004; Selig 2004, 613–20.
34 Schleusener 2004.
35 Koch 2006, 139.
36 „Antrag auf Genehmigung zur Errichtung oder Übernahme einer Verkaufsstelle", 27 Nov. 1939; StadtA Mü, Gewerbeamt, Abg. 7/12a.
37 Otto Bernheimer in: Familien- und Geschäftschronik 1950, 181–82.
38 Heuwagen 1987.
39 Petzet 1961, 35.
40 Gespräch mit \ Conversation with Konrad O. Bernheimer; Ernst Bernheimer in: Familien- und Geschäftschronik, 131.
41 Harburger 1998, III, 445, 480, 482, 503.
42 Durian-Ress 1991.
43 Gespräch mit \ Conversation with Konrad O. Bernheimer.
44 Bernheimer 1956, 91.
45 Stewart 1993, 165.
46 Ernst Bernheimer in: Familien- und Geschäftschronik, 73–74.
47 Göpel 1961, 81.
48 Sonderausstellung 1931.
49 Bachhofer 1931, 39.
50 Sarre 1912, Nrs. 13, 22, 43, 53, 63–64, 129, 163, 2648, 3016, 3023, 3216, 3217, 3242.
51 Ernst Bernheimer in: Familien- und Geschäftschronik 1950, 90–91.
52 Bernheimer 1956, 9.
53 Ernst Bernheimer in: Familien- und Geschäftschronik 1950, 93–94.
54 Feulner 1932.
55 Koch 2006, 138–39, 145 n. 69.
56 Sangl 2006, 321–22.
57 Bayerisches Nationalmuseum, Inventarblätter 51/10–51/13.
58 Powell 1954, 340.
59 Helbing 1930, lot 306; Ernst Bernheimer in: Familien- und Geschäftschronik 1950, 77.

Frédéric Eugène Piat
La Nature, Paris, 1900
Onyx, Bronze, Email
Sammlung Familie Bernheimer, Burg Marquartstein
Kat. Nr. 1

Frédéric Eugène Piat
La Nature, Paris, 1900
Onyx, bronze, enamel
Bernheimer Family Collection, Burg Marquartstein
Cat. no. 1

Textilfragmente
Florenz, Anfang 16. Jahrhundert
Velourbrokat, Seide, Gold und Silber broschiert
Sammlung Familie Bernheimer, Burg Marquartstein
Kat. Nr. 8

Textile Fragment
Florence, beginning of the 16th century
Velvet brocade, silk, embroidered with gold and silver threads
Bernheimer Family Collection, Burg Marquartstein
Cat. no. 8

Kissenbezug
Osmanisches Reich, Ende 16. Jahrhundert
Seide, broschiert
Sammlung Familie Bernheimer, Burg Marquartstein
Kat. Nr. 9

Cushion Cover
Ottoman Empire, end of the 16th century
Embroidered silk
Bernheimer Family Collection, Burg Marquartstein
Cat. no. 9

SAMMELBILDER **05** COLLECTING IMAGES

Bildteppich-Fragment „Wildleutepaar"
Basel, um 1480
Wolle
Schweizerisches Landesmuseum, Zürich
Kat. Nr. 10

Tapestry Fragment "Wild Couple"
Basel, c. 1480
Wool
Schweizerisches Landesmuseum, Zurich
Cat. no. 10

Bildteppich-Fragment „Frau sammelt Holunderblüten"
Basel, um 1470
Wolle, Leinen
Schweizerisches Landesmuseum, Zürich
Kat. Nr. 11

Tapestry Fragment "Woman Collecting Elder-blossoms"
Basel, c. 1470
Wool, linen
Schweizerisches Landesmuseum, Zurich
Cat. no. 11

„Holbeinstuhl"
Italien, 16. Jarhundert
Bezug: Fragment eines Knüpfteppichs,
Anatolien, 16. Jahrhundert
Sammlung Familie Bernheimer,
Burg Marquartstein
Kat. Nr. 5

"Holbein Chair"
Italy, 16th century
Upholstery: fragment of a 16th-century
Anatolian knotted carpet
Bernheimer Family Collection,
Burg Marquartstein
Cat. no. 5

Cassone (Truhe) mit „certosina" Technik
Italien, 16. Jahrhundert
Nußholz mit Fruchtholz-Intarsien
Sammlung Familie Bernheimer, Burg Marquartstein
Kat. Nr. 6

Cassone (Chest) with "Certosina" Technique
Italy, 16th century
Walnut with fruitwood intarsia
Bernheimer Family Collection, Burg Marquartstein
Cat. no. 6

DIE KUNST- UND ANTIQUITÄTENFIRMA BERNHEIMER \ THE ART AND ANTIQUES HOUSE OF BERNHEIMER

Buddha
Japan, 19. Jahrhundert
Holz, geschnitzt, schwarz gefasst
Sammlung Familie Bernheimer, Burg Marquartstein
Kat. Nr. 3

Buddha
Japan, 19th century
Carved and painted wood
Bernheimer Family Collection, Burg Marquartstein
Cat. no. 3

Aquamanile (Gießgefäß)
Lothringen, 12. Jahrhundert
Bronze
Landesmuseum Württemberg, Stuttgart
Kat. Nr. 7

Aquamanile (Ewer)
Lorraine, 12th century
Bronze
Landesmuseum Württemberg, Stuttgart
Cat. no. 7

Demonstrationsuhr
Deutschland, 1905
Deutsches Museum, München
Kat. Nr. 18

Demonstration Clock
Germany, 1905
Deutsches Museum, Munich
Cat. no. 18

Vase
Daum Frères & Cie
Nancy, um 1900/1905
Glas
Bayerisches Nationalmuseum,
München
Kat. Nr. 12

Vase
Daum Frères & Cie
Nancy, c. 1900/1905
Glass
Bayerisches Nationalmuseum,
Munich
Cat. no. 12

Vase
Josef Velik
Böhmen, um 1910
Glas
Bayerisches Nationalmuseum,
München
Kat. Nr. 13

Vase
Josef Velik
Bohemia, c. 1910
Glass
Bayerisches Nationalmuseum,
Munich
Cat. no. 13

Vase
René Lalique, Paris, 1921
Glas
Bayerisches Nationalmuseum, München
Kat. Nr. 14

Vase
René Lalique, Paris, 1921
Glass
Bayerisches Nationalmuseum, Munich
Cat. no. 14

Verzeichnis der Ausstellungsexponate
Checklist of Works Exhibited

Die Leihgaben stammen, wenn nicht anders angegeben, aus der
Sammlung Familie Bernheimer, Burg Marquartstein
All works have been lent by the Bernheimer Family Collection, Burg Marquartstein, unless otherwise indicated.

1 Abb. S. 39	**1** Fig. p. 39

<table>
<tr><td>

1   Abb. S. 39

Frédéric Eugène Piat (1827–1903)
La Nature, 1900
Onyx, Bronze, Email
H: 344 cm; D: 73 cm

Etwa 1900, erworben von Lehmann Bernheimer direkt von der „Exposition Universelle à Paris".
Lit.: *Paris Belle-Epoque*, Nr. 2

2

Amphore aus dem Treppenhaus Ottostraße
Frankreich, um 1880
Bronze
H: 120 cm; D: 70 cm

3   Abb. S. 45

Buddha
Japan, 19. Jahrhundert
Holz, geschnitzt, schwarz gefasst
H: 88 cm; B: 58 cm; T: 37 cm

4

Zwei große Wandleuchter (Engel mit Posaunen)
Frankreich, 19. Jahrhundert
Bronze, feuervergoldet
H: 70 cm; B: 45 cm; T: 70 cm

5   Abb. S. 43

„Holbeinstuhl"
Italien, 16. Jahrhundert
Bezug: Fragment eines sehr seltenen blaugrundigen Knüpfteppichs
Anatolien, 16. Jahrhundert
Wolle (sog. „Holbein-Teppich")
H: 160 cm; B: 73 cm; T: 60 cm
Lit.: *Bernheimer 1959*, Abb. 143

6   Abb. S. 44

Cassone (Truhe) in „certosina" Technik
Italien, 16. Jahrhundert
Nußholz mit Fruchtholz-Intarsien
H: 100 cm; B: 215; T: 73 cm

</td><td>

1   Fig. p. 39

Frédéric Eugène Piat (1827–1903)
La Nature, 1900
Onyx, bronze, enamel
H: 344 cm; W: 73 cm

Acquired c. 1900 by Lehmann Bernheimer directly from the "Exposition Universelle à Paris."
Lit.: *Paris Belle-Epoque*, no. 2

2

Amphora from the Ottostrasse Stairwell
France, c. 1880
Bronze
H: 120 cm; Diam: 70 cm

3   Fig. p. 45

Buddha
Japan, 19th century
Wood: carved with black pigment
H: 88 cm; W: 58 cm; D: 37 cm

4

Two Large Wall Sconces (Angels with Trumpets)
France, 19th century
Bronze: fire gilt
H: 70 cm; W: 45 cm; D: 70 cm

5   Fig. p. 43

"Holbein Chair"
Italian, 16th century
Upholstery: fragment of a very rare knotted carpet with blue field
Anatolia, 16th century
Wool (so-called "Holbein carpet")
H: 160 cm; W: 73 cm; D: 60 cm
Lit.: *Bernheimer 1959*, fig. 143

6   Fig. p. 44

Cassone (Chest) with "Certosina" Technique
Italy, 16th century
Walnut with fruitwood intarsia
H: 100 cm; W: 215 cm; D: 73 cm

</td></tr>
</table>

7 Abb. S. 46	**7** Fig. p. 46

7   Abb. S. 46

Aquamanile (Gießgefäß)
Lothringen, 12. Jahrhundert
Bronze
H: 14 cm; L: 16 cm
Landesmuseum Württemberg, Stuttgart, # 1960–350
(ehemals Bayerisches Nationalmuseum, München;
1951 Sammlung Otto Bernheimer im Tausch)

Lit.: *Weinmüller 1960*, Nr. 48b

8   Abb. S. 40

Textilfragmente
Florenz, Anfang 16. Jahrhundert
Zwei Bahnen Velourbrokat, Seide, Gold und Silber
broschiert, Granatapfelmuster
H: 160 cm; B: 116 cm
(ehemals Sammlung Otto Bernheimer)

Lit.: *Weinmüller 1960*, Nr. 461

9   Abb. S. 41

Kissenbezug
Osmanisches Reich, Ende 16. Jahrhundert
Seide, broschiert
H: 75 cm; B: 110 cm

10   Abb. S. 42

Bildteppich-Fragment „Wildleutepaar"
Basel, um 1480
Wolle
H: 48,5 cm; B: 41,5 cm
Schweizerisches Landesmuseum, Zürich, # LM 29306
(ehemals Sammlung Otto Bernheimer)

Lit.: *Kurth 1931*, 236-237, Abb. 3; *Weinmüller 1960*, Nr. 354a;
Rapp Buri 1990, 199, Nr. 40

11   Abb. S. 42

**Bildteppich-Fragment
„Frau sammelt Holunderblüten"**
Basel, um 1470
Wolle, Leinen
H: 44 cm; B: 52 cm
Schweizerisches Landesmuseum, Zürich, # LM 29307
(ehemals Sammlung Otto Bernheimer)

Lit.: *Kurth 1931*, 237-238, Abb. 4; *Weinmüller 1960*, Nr. 354b;
Rapp Buri 1990, 192, Nr. 35

---

7   Fig. p. 46

Aquamanile (Ewer)
Lorraine, 12th century
Bronze
H: 14 cm; W: 16 cm
Landesmuseum Württemberg, Stuttgart, # 1960-350
(formerly Bayerisches Nationalmuseum;
1951 Otto Bernheimer, by exchange)

Lit.: *Weinmüller 1960*, no. 48b

8   Fig. p. 40

Textile Fragment
Florence, beginning of the 16th century
Two widths of velvet brocade, silk: embroidered with
gold and silver threads; pomegranate motif
H: 160 cm; W: 116 cm
(formerly Otto Bernheimer collection)

Lit.: *Weinmüller 1960*, no. 461

9   Fig. p. 41

Cushion Cover
Ottoman Empire, end of the 16th century
Silk: embroidered
H: 75 cm; W: 110 cm

10   Fig. p. 42

Tapestry Fragment "Wild Couple"
Basel, c. 1480
Wool
H: 48.5 cm; W: 41.5 cm
Schweizerisches Landesmuseum, Zürich, # LM 29306
(formerly Otto Bernheimer collection)

Lit.: *Kurth 1931*, 236-237, fig. 3; *Weinmüller 1960*, no. 354a;
Rapp Buri 1990, 199, no. 40

11   Fig. p. 42

**Tapestry Fragment
"Woman Collecting Elder-blossoms"**
Basel, c. 1470
Wool, linen
H: 44 cm; W: 52 cm
Schweizerisches Landesmuseum, Zürich, # LM 29307
(formerly Otto Bernheimer collection)

Lit.: *Kurth 1931*, 237-38, fig. 4; *Weinmüller 1960*, no. 354b;
Rapp Buri 1990, 192, no. 35

12 Abb. S. 48	**12** Fig. p. 48
Vase	**Vase**
Daum Frères & Cie; E. Mottheau (Fuß)	Daum Frères & Cie; E. Mottheau (base)
Nancy, um 1900/1905	Nancy, c. 1900/1905
Glas, überfangen, polychrom, geätzt,	Glass: layered, polychrome, acid-etched;
Bronze patiniert (Fuß)	patinated bronze (base)
H: 29,5 cm	H: 29.5 cm
Bayerisches Nationalmuseum, München, # L 96/25	Bayerisches Nationalmuseum, Munich, # L 96/25
(ehemals Sammlung Otto Bernheimer)	(formerly Otto Bernheimer collection)

Lit.: *Weinmüller 1960*, Nr. 19

Lit.: *Weinmüller 1960*, no. 19

13 Abb. S. 48

Vase
Josef Velik
Kosten bei Teplitz (Kostany u Teplic), Böhmen, um 1910
Glas, gefärbt, violett, Einschmelzungen, irisiert
H: 29,5 cm
Bayerisches Nationalmuseum, München, # L 96/31
(ehemals Sammlung Otto Bernheimer)

13 Fig. p. 48

Vase
Josef Velik
Kostany u Teplic, Bohemia, c. 1910
Glass: colored violet, molten applications, iridescence
H: 29.5 cm
Bayerisches Nationalmuseum, Munich, # L 96/31
(formerly Otto Bernheimer collection)

14 Abb. S. 49

Vase
René Lalique (1860–1945)
Paris, 1921
Glas, preßluftgeblasen, geätzt, patiniert, geschliffen
H: 26,5 cm; D: 10,2 cm (Boćen); D: 9,9 cm (Mündung)
Bayerisches Nationalmuseum, München # L 96/27
(ehemals Sammlung Otto Bernheimer)

14 Fig. p. 49

Vase
René Lalique (1860–1945)
Paris, 1921
Glass: compressed-air-blown, acid-etched, patinated, polished
H: 26.5 cm; Diam: 10.2 cm (base); Diam: 9.9 cm (mouth)
Bayerisches Nationalmuseum, Munich, # L 96/27
(formerly Otto Bernheimer collection)

15

Chorgestühl-Fragmente aus der Münchner Frauenkirche
Werkstatt des Erasmus Grasser, München, um 1502
Gewölbe mit Rippen, Schnitzwerk, Eiche
H: 320 cm; B: 220 cm; T: 50 cm (unten), 80 cm (oben)
Münchner Stadtmuseum, # M 71/189
(Geschenk Otto Bernheimer, 1958)

15

Choir Stalls (Fragment) from Munich's Frauenkirche
Workshop of Erasmus Grasser, Munich, c. 1502
Oak: carved; ribbed vaults
H: 320 cm; W: 220 cm; D: 50 cm (bottom), 80 cm (top)
Münchner Stadtmuseum, # M 71/189
(Gift of Otto Bernheimer, 1958)

Provenienz: Karl Theodor von Piloty (nach 1859); Eduard v. Grützner (1866); L. Bernheimer (1930)

Provenance: Karl Theodor von Piloty (after 1859); Eduard v. Grützner (1866); L. Bernheimer (1930)

Lit.: *Helbing 1930*, Nr. 306; *Hoh-Slodczyk 1985*, 51ff.; *Breyer 1993*; *Otto 1994*

Lit.: *Helbing 1930*, no. 306; *Hoh-Slodczyk 1985*, 51ff.; *Breyer 1993*; *Otto 1994*

16	**Rüböl-Lampe** Marokko, 19. Jahrhundert Messing H: 77,5 cm; D: 31 cm Deutsches Museum, München, # 1910-25269 (Geschenk von Lehmann Bernheimer, 1910)	16	**Rapeseed Oil Lamp** Morocco, 19th century Brass H: 77.5 cm; Diam: 31 cm Deutsches Museum, Munich, # 1910-25269 (Gift of Lehmann Bernheimer, 1910)
17	**Zerlegbarer Ofen** Deutschland, 1801–25 Fayence H: 52 cm; B: 40 cm; T: 60 cm Deutsches Museum, München, # 1909-20601 (Geschenk von Lehmann Bernheimer, 1909)	17	**Portable Oven** Germany, 1801–25 Faience H: 52 cm; W: 40 cm; D: 60 cm Deutsches Museum, Munich, # 1909-20601 (Gift of Lehmann Bernheimer, 1909)
18	Abb. S. 47 **Demonstrationsuhr** Sign.: August Bacher Deutschland, 1905 Skelettierte Standuhr in Holzgehäuse mit Unruh und Gewichtsaufzug H: 135 cm; B: 35 cm; T: 23 cm Deutsches Museum, München, # 1905-2234 (Geschenk von Lehmann Bernheimer, 1905)	18	Fig. p. 47 **Demonstration Clock** Sign.: August Bacher Germany, 1905 Skeleton floor clock in a wood cabinet with balance wheel and counterweight H: 135 cm; W: 35 cm; D: 23 cm Deutsches Museum, Munich, # 1905-2234 (Gift of Lehmann Bernheimer, 1905)
19	**Entwurf der Einrichtungsabteilung des Hauses Bernheimer durch den hauseigenen Architekten Ferber** München, vor 1938 Aquarell H: 42,5 cm; B: 36,5 cm	19	**Design for an Interior by Bernheimer's Furnishings Department House Architect Ferber** Munich, before 1938 Watercolor H: 42.5 cm; W: 36.5 cm
20	Abb. S. 21 **Entwurf der Einrichtungsabteilung des Hauses Bernheimer durch den hauseigenen Architekten Ferber** München, vor 1938 Tempera H: 46 cm; B: 57 cm	20	Fig. p. 21 **Design for an Interior by Bernheimer's Furnishings Department House Architect Ferber** Munich, before 1938 Tempera H: 46 cm; W: 57 cm

21	Abb. S. 22	21	Fig. p. 22

21   Abb. S. 22

Entwurf für eine private Kappelle, Entwurf der Einrichtungsabteilung des Hauses Bernheimer durch den hauseigenen Architekten Ferber
München, vor 1938
Aquarell, Collage auf Pappe
H: 23 cm; B: 28,8 cm

22

Entwurf der Einrichtungsabteilung des Hauses Bernheimer durch den hauseigenen Architekten Ferber
München, 1910
Aquarell auf Pappe
H: 30,5 cm; B: 48 cm

23

Musterbuch mit dem Angebot an Textilien zur Inneneinrichtung
(Signatur am Buchrücken: 1-1512)
München, vor 1938
H: 44,5 cm; B: 33 cm

24

Musterbuch mit dem Angebot an Möbeln
„Stilmöbel: Renaissance mit Barock"
München, vor 1938
H: 45 cm; B: 38 cm

25

Musterbuch mit dem Angebot an Möbeln
„Kommoden, Kredenzen, Konsolen"
München, vor 1938
H: 45 cm; B: 38 cm

26   Abb. S. 18

Auswahl von Zierleisten
die in der Gestaltung von Inneneinrichtungen eingesetzt werden konnten.

27

Auswahl an Metallgriffen, montiert auf einer Holzplatte
H: 66 cm; B: 18 cm

---

21   Fig. p. 22

Design for a Private Chapel by Bernheimer's Furnishings Department House Architect Ferber
Munich, before 1938
Watercolor and collage on board
H: 23 cm; W: 28.8 cm

22

Design for an Interior by Bernheimer's Furnishings Department House Architect Ferber
Munich, 1910
Watercolor on board
H: 30.5 cm; W: 48 cm

23

Catalog Book with Textile Samples for Interior Decoration
(Book number on spine: 1-1512)
Munich, before 1938
H: 44.5 cm; W: 33 cm

24

Catalog Book with Furniture Collections
"Period Furniture: Renaissance and Baroque"
Munich, before 1938
H: 45 cm; W: 38 cm

25

Catalog Book with Furniture Collections
"Commodes, Sideboards, Consoles"
Munich, before 1938
H: 45 cm; W: 38 cm

26   Fig. p. 18

Selection of Decorative Moldings
For use in interiors designed by the Bernheimer firm

27

Selection of Metal Handles, mounted on a wood board
H: 66 cm; W: 18 cm

28
Karteikarten zu den Objekten aus dem Bestand der Firma L. Bernheimer
„Sitzmöbel: Empire und Biedermeier"
Fotografien auf Karton collagiert
H: 10 cm; B: 42 cm; T: 30 cm

29   Abb. S. 14
Franz von Lenbach (1836–1904)
Studie für das *Porträt Lehmann Bernheimers*, 1903
Öl auf Pappe
H: 55,5 cm; B: 40 cm
Städtische Galerie im Lenbachhaus, München, # L 634
Lit.: *Mehl 1980*, 123, Nr. 232.

30
Trauer-Gedenkbuch „dem Andenken meines unvergesslichen Vaters Lehmann Bernheimer gewidmet. Sterbetag am 29. Mai 1918, 18. Siwan 5678 im 77. Lebensjahre"
Verlag für Trauerbücher, Berlin, W. 50. Ansbacherstr. 35.

31   Abb. S. 29
„Auf der Suche nach der verlorenen Zeit"
Titelseite der Zeitschrift „Der Spiegel",
25. Dezember 1957
Hamburg, 1957
Privatbesitz, München

32   Abb. S. 15
„L. Bernheimer, München, Kaufingerstraße. Möbelstoffe und Teppiche …"
Arnold & Zettler, München, 1879
Anzeige, Druck, gerahmt
H: 67 cm; B: 51 cm

33   Abb. S. 16
Einweihung des italienischen Hofs des Palais Bernheimer durch Prinzregent Luitpold
München, 1910
Fotografie
H: 28,5 cm; B: 22,5 cm

28
Catalog Cards for Objects in the Inventory of the Firm L. Bernheimer
"Furniture for Seating: Empire and Biedermeier"
Photographs glued onto cardboard
H: 10 cm; W: 42 cm; D: 30 cm

29   Fig. p. 14
Franz von Lenbach (1836–1904)
Study for the *Portrait of Lehmann Bernheimer*, 1903
Oil on board
H: 55.5 cm; W: 40 cm
Städtische Galerie im Lenbachhaus, Munich, # L 634
Lit.: *Mehl 1980*, 123, no. 232

30
Mourning-Memorial Book "dedicated to the memory of my never-to-be-forgotten father Lehmann Bernheimer. Died on May 29, 1918, 18th of Sivan 5678 at the age of 77"
Verlag für Trauerbucher, Berlin, W. 50 Ansbacherstr. 35.

31   Fig. p. 29
"In Search of Lost Time"
Cover of the periodical *Der Spiegel*,
December 25, 1957
Hamburg, 1957
Private Collection, Munich

32   Fig. p. 15
"L. Bernheimer, Munich, Kaufingerstrasse. Upholstery Fabrics and Carpets…"
Arnold & Zettler, Munich, 1879
Printed advertisement, framed
H: 67 cm; W: 51 cm

33   Fig. p. 16
Dedication of the Italian Court in the Bernheimer Palais by Prince Regent Luitpold
Munich, 1910
Photograph
H: 28.5 cm; W: 22.5 cm

34		34	
	Abb. S. 23		Fig. p. 23

34 — Abb. S. 23
Mitarbeiter der Firma Bernheimer im italienischen Hof des Palais Bernheimer
München, 1914
Fotografie
H: 16 cm; B: 21,9 cm
In der ersten Reihe Lehmann Bernheimer mit seinen drei Söhnen Max, Ernst und Otto

35
Firmenschilder der Firma Bernheimer
a) Exklusive Einrichtungen:
Stoffe, Tapeten, Teppichböden, Polstermöbel, Einzelmöbel
München, um 1950/1955
Hinterglas-Beschriftung
H: 59 cm; B: 46 cm

b) Antiquitäten:
Kunstgegenstände des 16.–19. Jahrhundert,
Antike Möbel, Teppiche, Tapisserien, Skulpturen, Gemälde, Chinesische Kunst
München, um 1950/1955
Hinterglas-Beschriftung
H: 59 cm; B: 46 cm

36
Messestandschild „Bernheimer München 16"
Standschild bei der ersten Deutschen Kunstmesse 1956 im Haus der Kunst
Angefertigt von den eigenen Werkstätten des Hauses Bernheimer am Lenbachplatz 3
Holz, bemalt
H: 68 cm; B: 46 cm

37
„Des Vaters Segen baut den Kindern Häuser. Zum 27. Dezember 1916"
Bernheimer Stationen
C. Haesecke, 1916
15 Fotografien, retouchiert
H: 40,1 cm; B: 50,2 cm

34 — Fig. p. 23
Personnel of the Bernheimer Firm in the Italian Court of the Bernheimer Palais
Munich, 1914
Photograph
H: 16 cm; W: 21.9 cm
Seated in the first row are Lehmann Bernheimer and his three sons Max, Ernst, and Otto

35
Company Signs of the Bernheimer Firm
a) Exclusive Furnishings: Fabrics, Wallpaper, Carpets, Upholstered Furniture, Individual Pieces of Furniture
Munich, c. 1950/1955
Hinterglas lettering
(painted on the reverse side of the glass)
H: 59 cm; W: 46 cm

b) Antiques: Artworks of the 16th–19th centuries, Antique Furniture, Carpets, Tapestries, Sculpture, Paintings, Chinese Art
Munich, c. 1950/1955
Hinterglas lettering
(painted on the reverse side of the glass)
H: 59 cm; W: 46 cm

36
Exhibition Stand Sign "Bernheimer Munich 16"
For the first German Art Fair at Haus der Kunst in 1956
Made by Bernheimer's in-house workshop at Lenbachplatz 3
Wood: painted
H: 68 cm; W: 46 cm

37
"The Father's Blessing Builds the Children's Homes. On the Occasion of December 27, 1916"
Bernheimer Stations
C. Haesecke, 1916
15 retouched photographs
H: 40.1 cm; W: 50.2 cm

Bibliographie
Bibliography

Bachhofer 1931 = Bachhofer, Ludwig: An Exhibition of Siamese Sculpture in Munich, in: The Burlington Magazine for Connoisseurs, Vol. 59, No. 340 (July 1931), 34, 38-39.

Baedeker 1914 = Baedeker, Karl: Southern Germany. Handbook for Travellers. Leipzig, London and New York 1914.

Baedeker 1925 = Südbayern. Handbuch für Reisende von Karl Baedeker, 37. Auflage, Leipzig 1925.

Bauer, Ingolf: Keramik handwerklicher Herstellung, in: Renate Eikelmann; Ingolf Bauer (Hg.): Das Bayerische Nationalmuseum 1855–2005. 150 Jahre Sammeln, Forschen, Ausstellen. München 2006, 592-610.

Bernheimer 1929 = Bernheimer, Ludwig: Die Rechtsverhältnisse der an einer Kunstversteigerung beteiligten Personen. München 1929.

Bernheimer 1956 = Bernheimer, Otto: Erinnerungen eines alten Münchners. München 1956.

Bernheimer 1959 = Bernheimer, Otto: Alte Teppiche des 16. bis 18. Jahrhunderts der Firma L. Bernheimer. München 1959.

Bernheimer. Zurück zum Barock, in: Der Spiegel, 25. Dezember 1957, 42-50.

Breyer 1993 = Breyer, Heinrich: Die Odyssee eines Altmünchner Chorgestühls, in: Süddeutsche Zeitung, 24./25./26. Dezember 1993.

Christie's South Kensington: The Bernheimer Family Collection of Liturgical Vestments. Auction Catalogue, 2 October 1996. London 1996.

Dornberg, John: A new home for Bernheimer, in: Art and Auction, Sept. 21 – Oct. 4, 1998, Vol. 21, No. 2, 26-28.

Durian-Ress 1991 = Durian-Ress, Saskia: Textilien Sammlung Bernheimer. Paramente 15.-19. Jahrhundert. München 1991.

Erste Deutsche Kunst- und Antiquitäten Messe München. Haus der Kunst. München 1956.

Familien- und Geschäftschronik 1950 = Bernheimer, Ernst: Familien- und Geschäftschronik der Firma L. Bernheimer K.-G., mit Beiträge von Karoline Bernheimer und Otto Bernheimer. München 1950.

Feulner 1932 = Feulner, Adolf: Ein Meisterwerk dekorativer Louis XVI-Malerei, in: Pantheon. Monatsschrift für Freunde und Sammler der Kunst, Bd. 9 (1932), 133-137.

Förster, Christina M.: Der Harnier-Kreis. Widerstand gegen den Nationalsozialismus in Bayern. Paderborn 1996.

Friedländer 1997 = Friedländer, Saul: Nazi Germany and the Jews. The Years of Persecution 1933–39. London 1997.

Gaehtgens 1993 = Gaehtgens, Thomas W.: Wilhelm von Bode und seine Sammler, in: Ekkehard Mai; Peter Paret (Hg.): Sammler, Stifter und Museen – Kunstförderung in Deutschland im 19. und 20. Jahrhundert. Köln, Weimar, Wien 1993, 153-172.

Göpel 1961 = Göpel, Erhard: Schätze aus Orient und Okzident. Die Nachlaß-Versteigerung Konsul Otto Bernheimer in München bringt 2 Millionen Mark, in: Madame, Februar 1961, 81-85.

Harburger 1998 = Harburger, Theodor: Die Inventarisation jüdischer Kunst- und Kulturdenkmäler in Bayern. 3 Bde. Fürth-Jerusalem 1998.

Helbing 1930 = Helbing, Hugo: Sammlung Eduard v. Grützner München, Auktionskatalog (Versteigerungshaus Hugo Helbing, München), 24. Juni 1930.

Heusler, Weger 1998 = Heusler, Andreas; Weger, Tobias: „Kristallnacht". Gewalt gegen die Münchner Juden im November 1938. München 1998.

Heuwagen 1987 = Heuwagen, Marianne: „Bayerisch sind wir noch". Ein Kapitel aus der Bernheimer-Story, in: Süddeutsche Zeitung, 24./25. Januar 1987, 187.

Hoh-Slodczyk 1985 = Hoh-Slodczyk, Christine: Das Haus des Künstlers im 19. Jahrhundert. München 1985.

Juden in Buttenhausen. Ständige Ausstellung in der Bernheime'schen Realschule Buttenhausen, bearbeitet von Roland Deigendeschl. Münsingen 1994.

Kassel, Neue Galerie, Staatliche und Städtische Kunstsammlungen Kassel: Franz Bernheimer. Zeichnungen und Aquarelle 1955–1981. Kassel 1983.

Koch 2006 = Koch, Michael: Das Bayerische Nationalmuseum unter Hans Buchheit 1932–1947, in: Renate Eikelmann; Ingolf Bauer (Hg.): Das Bayerische Nationalmuseum 1855–2005. 150 Jahre Sammeln, Forschen, Ausstellen. München 2006, 132-147.

Konstantin Prinz von Bayern 1956 = Konstantin Prinz von Bayern: Die großen Namen. Begegnungen mit bedeutenden Deutschen unserer Zeit. München 1956.

Krauss, Marita: Familiengeschichte als Zeitgeschichte. Die jüdischen Familien Bernheimer, Feuchtwanger und Rosenfeld in Nationalsozialismus und Nachkriegszeit, in: Archiv für Familiengeschichtsforschung, 9 (1997), 3, 162-176.

Küppers, Jean: Ein Begriff für exklusive Einrichtung: Bernheimer München, in: Die Kunst und das schöne Heim, 82 (1970), 111-113.

Kurth 1931 = Kurth, Betty: Vier unbekannte Schweizer Bildwirkerein, in: Pantheon. Monatsschrift für Freunde und Sammler der Kunst, Bd. 6 (1931), 234-238.

Leber, Marianne: Das Haus Bernheimer, in: Das Bayerland, 62 (1960), 447-452.

MGR: Bernheimer stiftet ein Chorgestühl, in: Süddeutscher Zeitung, 9. Juni 1958.

Mehl 1980 = Mehl, Sonja: Franz von Lenbach in der Städtischen Galerie in Lenbachhaus München. München 1980.

Morris 1915 = Morris, Frances: A Recent Accession of Ecclesiastical Vestments, in: The Metropolitan Museum of Art Bulletin, 10 (1915), 47-49.

Müller-Mehlis, Reinhard: Bernheimer und München. Gedanken zur Familiengeschichte, in: Kunst und Tradition. Meisterwerke bedeutender Provenienzen. München 1989, 19-24.

Netzer, Nancy; Reinburg, Virginia (eds.): Fragmented Devotion. Medieval Objects from the Schnütgen Museum Cologne. Boston 2000.

Neumeier, Gerhard: Bürgerliches Mäzenatentum in München vor dem Ersten Weltkrieg – Das Beispiel des Deutschen Museums, in: Jürgen Kocka; Manuel Frey (Hg.): Bürgerkultur und Mäzenatentum im 19. Jahrhundert, Berlin 1998, 144-163.

Otto 1994 = Otto, Kornelius: Das Chorgestühl der Frauenkirche im Wandel der Zeit, in: Hans Ramisch (Hg.): Monachium Sacrum. Festschrift zur 500-Jahr-Feier der Metropolitankirche zu unserer Lieben Frau in München, Band II (Kunstgeschichte). München 1994, 303-376.

Page, Amy: Textiles au fil des ventes, in: Connaissance des Arts, no. 529 (1996), 108-113.

Paret, Peter: Bemerkungen zu dem Thema: Jüdische Kunstsammler, Stifter und Kunsthändler, in: Ekkehard Mai; Peter Paret (Hg.): Sammler, Stifter und Museen – Kunstförderung in Deutschland im 19. und 20. Jahrhundert. Köln, Weimar, Wien 1993, 173-185.

Paris, Belle-Epoque = Paris, Belle-Epoque: 1880–1914. Kunsthalle der Hypo-Kulturstiftung München. München 1994.

Petropoulos, Jonathan: The Faustian Bargain. The Art World in Nazi Germany. London 2000.

Petzet 1961 = Petzet, Wolfgang: Münchens Zwei-Millionen-Auktion, in: Münchner Leben. Monatzeitschrift für Gesellschaft, Kommunalpolitik, Kunst und Wirtschaft, 1/1961, 35-39.

Pfeiffer-Belli, Erich: Hundert Jahre Bernheimer. München 1964.

Powell 1954 = Powell, Nicolas: Notes on German Art Collections since 1945, in: The Burlington Magazine, Vol. 96, No. 620 (Nov. 1954), 338-344.

Rapp Buri 1990 = Rapp Buri, Anna; Stucky-Schürer, Monica: Zahm und Wild – Basler und Straßburger Bildtepppiche des 15. Jahrhunderts, Mainz 1990.

Sangl 2006 = Sangl, Sigrid: Decken, Vertäfelungen und Kabinette, in: Renate Eikelmann; Ingolf Bauer (Hg.): Das Bayerische Nationalmuseum 1855–2005. 150 Jahre Sammeln, Forschen, Ausstellen. München 2006, 315-325.

Sarre 1912 = Sarre, F.; Martin, F. R. (Hg.): Die Ausstellung von Meisterwerken muhammedanischer Kunst in München 1910, 3 Bde. München 1912.

Schleusener 2004 = Schleusener, Jan: Vom Kunsthändler zum Kaffeebauer. Ausschaltung und Emigration am Beispiel Bernheimer, in: Zeitenblicke 3 (2004), Nr. 2, [13.09.2004], URL: http://zeitenblicke.historicum.net/2004/02/schleusener/index.html.

Selig 2004 = Selig, Wolfram: „Arisierung" in München. Die Vernichtung jüdischer Existenz 1937–1939. Berlin 2004.

Siebel, Ernst: Der großbürgerliche Salon 1850–1918. Geselligkeit und Wohnkultur. Berlin 1999.

Sonderausstellung 1931 = Sonderausstellung von Khmer und Siamplastiken, L. Bernheimer, München [1931].

Spuhler, Friedrich: Orientteppiche aus dem Hause Bernheimer, heute im Museum für Islamische Kunst Berlin, in: Kunst und Tradition. Meisterwerke bedeutender Provenienzen. München 1989, 25-28.

Stewart 1993 = Stewart, Susan: On Longing. Narratives of the Miniature, the Gigantic, the Souvenir, the Collection. Durham, London 1993.

Winstel, Tobias: "Healed Biographies"? Jewish Remigration and Indemnification for National Socialist Injustice, in: Leo Baeck Institute Yearbook, 49 (2004), 137-152.

Archivalische Quellen
Archival Sources

Bayerisches Nationalmuseum:
– Dokumentation, Dok. 1160, Schachtel 25
– Dokumentation, Dok. 1439, Schachtel 31
– Inventarblätter

Bayerische Staatsgemäldesammlung:
– Beschlagnahmungslisten der Gemälde

Münchner Stadtmuseum:
– Registratur, Aktenkonvolut „Ehemaliger Judenbesitz"

Privatarchiv Familie Bernheimer, Burg Marquartstein

Stadtarchiv München:
– Personenmeldebögen (PMB) B 219
– Gewerbeamt (GA) Abg. 7/12a Bernheimer
– Zeitungsarchiv (ZA) Pers. Bernheimer

Abbildungsnachweis
Illustration Credits

Umschlag \ Cover, 15, 18, 21-23, 39-41, 43-45
Sammlung Familie Bernheimer, Burg Marquartstein, Foto: Dirk Spath

12, 16, 27 (unten \ bottom), 30
Erinnerungen eines alten Münchners. Erzählt von Otto Bernheimer, München 1957

14
Städtische Galerie im Lenbachhaus, München

17
Werbeheft: Die Firma L. Bernheimer in München, Lenbachplatz 3 und Ottostraße, S. 14, 15 und 16

27 (oben \ top)
Stadtarchiv München

29
Privatbesitz, München

31
Museum für Kunst und Gewerbe, Hamburg

32
Central Archives for the History of the Jewish People, Jerusalem, #160/848

33
Karl-Heinz Meissner, München

35
Diözesan-Museum, Freising, Wolf-Christian von der Mülbe

37, 48, 49
Bayerisches Nationalmuseum, München

42
Schweizerisches Landesmuseum, Zürich

46
Landesmuseum Württemberg, Stuttgart

47
Deutsches Museum, München

„… ob Truhe, Teppich, Relief oder Bronze, dahinter stand meistens: Bernheimer, München. Bernheimer, Papst unter den Kunstgläubigen."

"… whether chest, carpet, relief or bronze, behind these works there usually stood: Bernheimer, Munich. Bernheimer, Pope among art's true believers."

Konstantin, Prinz von Bayern: Die großen Namen. Begegnungen mit bedeutenden Deutschen unserer Zeit. München 1956, 24.